Hot mama

IN (HIGH) HEELS

Compiled by
CHRISTINE MARMOY

Coaching and Success
c/o Marketing for Coach, Ltd
Second Floor
6th London Street
W2 1HR London

www.coachingandsuccess.com
info@coachingandsuccess.com

ISBN: 978-0-9575561-2-6

Published in UK, Europe, US, Canada and Australia

Book cover and Inside Layout:
Karine St-Onge
www.shinyrocketdesign.com

TABLE OF CONTENTS

Thank You

Over the past few months, I have pondered a lot (and still do) the term "thank you." A little courtesy saying that we teach our children and that we were once told is that we shouldn't forget to thank everybody... or else!

In the context of this book, it is of course adequate to pay my tribute to all the persons who helped me put this book together, which I won't fail to do in a moment, but right now I'd like to take the opportunity to hold your hand and help you contemplate with me what exists beyond this everyday good manner.

Thank you is the doorway to accepting, to forgiving, and to receiving, whatever it might be. It didn't appear in our culture out of thin air, but rather from a very deep knowledge transcending all cultures and time. The term means more than what meets the eye.

"Thank you" needs to be used more often and without any expectation in return. I like to thank the Universe for everything that enters or leaves my life, from the breakfast I have on my terrace facing the sea each morning to my little cherry tomatoes growing peacefully on the same terrace, the smile I see on my baby's face, or all the clients coming to me to achieve their dreams.

"Thank you" means more than just that! Remember, it's a practice: Be thankful today for what you have so you can be ten times more thankful tomorrow.

Now, with that being said, I cannot possibly cover the entire subject of thankfulness in this little page, so let's walk the walk together and start the orchestrated gratitude that I'm so impatient to share with you.

First and foremost, I'd like to thank all the co-authors who contributed in this book; they shared very intimate stories that will touch your heart, just like they touched mine. They go all out, they are transparent, and they tell you how it is at face value. Thank you all for being so generous with your chapters.

Of course I couldn't conceive of thanking everybody, but I must thank my loving executive assistant Jane Bell. By now you surely know that she is the heart of it all; without her, I couldn't do what I do and I wouldn't be where I am right now.

Thank you to all my technical staff, who always thrive to make every single request a very special task that they complete like masters.

I am also so grateful to be working with Karine St-Onge, my graphic designer, whose artistic talents make all my projects so easy to showcase. She has a gift, and I am very glad that she uses it to help me be the best I can be.

Last but not least, thanks to all my clients, my Facebook followers, and my friends who trust me and who help me grow as a business and most importantly as a human being. All of you bring me so much in return.

Could I conclude this "Thank You" page without a word to my family? Absolutely not! I might have the craziest family that exists, but I wouldn't trade them for anything. They all drive me out of my mind at times, but they are also so proud of me that the stars in their eyes erase all the challenges. Thank you to my husband Pascal, who allowed me the time and the space to compile this book; to my daughter Camille for taking care of her little brother Mathys; and to my son Justyn for teaching me how to be "zen and patient" every day.

Compiled by **Christine Marmoy**

Introduction

When I first got the idea for this book, my deep desire was to bring together a wide range of women from different backgrounds, walks of life, experiences, statuses, careers, ethnicities, and spiritual practices in order to ensure that the book would be read and appreciated by ALL women in the world who had the chance to get their hands on it.

My vision was to allow *Hot Mama in (High) Heels* to become your favorite book—the one kept on your bedside table—as a written guide toward which you are drawn whenever something goes wrong, whenever you feel low and downhearted, whenever you need a nice, gentle kick in the butt, or whenever you want to feel even *better* than you do at that particular moment.

However, my vision was merely a shortcoming of what this book ended up becoming. It's a real tribute, a prayer with many verses, a compass for those who are lost, a fluffy pillow for those who need to rest their weary heads, a warm blanket for those who feel cold, a shoulder to lean on, a guide with many different voices and many different faces, but more importantly than all that, it is tangible proof of love.

Each word is a loving kiss, each line is a song emanating directly from the co-author's heart, each chapter is a testimonial to the fact that life can be wonderful if you choose it to be and can be easy when you know how to navigate your way through the rocks, across the currents and the fallen branches that sometimes get strewn across the river that represents the flow of life.

What struck me most of all when I read the chapters (yes, I do read everything I publish!) is that every single soul in this book is willing to share how much in the dark they once were, how far they went to try and hide away and to make themselves as small and invisible as possible from the world. So small, in fact, that they couldn't reach that special little place reserved for them in life until the Universe could finally no longer accept this situation. It reacted by giving them a fierce shake to wake them up and make them realize that life is not about hiding or about being like everybody else or whatever they imagined they should be; it's not about complaining or feeling victimized, but instead about shining your light, standing up for yourself, believing in yourself, staking your special big meaningful place in this world— about being YOURSELF!

And let me tell you, you don't need a reason to claim that place which is there for the taking and which, by the way, is empty and useless until you decide you are ready to occupy it. You don't need to be able to cover an entire wall with diplomas to retain that right; you don't need to get authorization, you don't need to go through 10 years of therapy, and you don't need to fear anything in order to reveal your true self and be the amazing and magnificent being that you are. All you need to do is recognize who you are and that you should live every second of every minute of every day in accordance with this universal truth— that you are a perfect human being, a wonderful WOMAN.

Now, I am not by any means implying that you or me, for that matter, are "perfect" as defined by the dictionary, but rather perfect in a divine way: perfect intrinsically. At that level, perfection does exist; it is just the meaning we apply to it that differs.

Each chapter in this book brought tears to my eyes, as well as a smile to my face—I even found myself nodding in agreement more than once. You'll probably do the same, and understandably so, as we've all felt the same way at some point or other in our lives. Sure enough, you will recognize yourself in the lines that follow just as much as I recognized myself.

When we first ventured out on this project, I asked all the wonderful ladies who contributed to this masterpiece to be as honest as possible and to give a part of themselves to you, my dear readers. They truly over-delivered on that request! Reading this book will propel you into an adventurous journey inside: You will reconnect with certain feelings you thought were gone forever and out of reach, you will recall episodes in your own life and suddenly a light will appear to illuminate the darkness in your mind, and you will understand and embrace the power of forgiveness and acceptance. You will ultimately drop that heavy load, the burden of your sorrow or the uneasiness you have had to carry within your heart until now. You will find the strength to move on with your life and to tap into that huge ocean of wisdom and happiness that makes life flow. This flow can only truly be seen when we are aligned; it is always there, in its tranquility as well as its strength as a rock. However, most of us spend the majority of our life blindfolded in the face of this evidence! We are not taught this at school, and for most of us it was not even discussed at home during supper time.

Nevertheless, it exists, and its power is unquestionable and undeniable.

The only question I may ask of you is: Are you ready? Are you ready to open your mind to the possibility that you too can make a complete 180° U-turn in your life as you know it right now in order to allow yourself to step into your own power and gain access to joy, peace, success, and contentment?

It is said today—at least the great thinkers, movers, or shakers in today's society agree about the fact—that we as women are destined to be the originators of newfound hope to help turn the tides of the world—be it in economics, politics, or education. The actual domain matters less than the fact that we are being called on to play a much bigger role in this world. This will subsequently have an impact on the way our children and all future generations live their lives and especially the kind of world they will be obliged to live in.

A pretty big task in hand, don't you think?

Although I firmly believe these kinds of statements to be true, I still hold in my heart the conviction that it is more about our feminine energy and how it translates in terms of the way we tackle things, solve issues, perceive life and engage in many other aspects rather than the mere fact of our female gender.

Today, I can honestly say that this feminine energy has no right to be or exist without its counterpart—in this case, the male energy. In other words, yes, we can be called upon to carry out that big task, but it will only be possible through feminine energy, not just through our female gender. This approach allows this concept plenty of room for our male counterparts to come to terms with reconciling their feminine power into their masculine body. And as a result, together we will achieve greatness. It is not a question of the disappearance of one power, but rather the integration and "tango" that both sides can dance together—it just means that the lead dancer is changing hands.

And obviously, all of us as women need to step up to the plate. How on earth can we help shape a better world for the generations to come when we cannot even shape a better one even closer to home: our own!

Think of this book as a small step toward achieving that goal, to help you refocus on what is important and help you understand how to become the leader in your own life, just as if you were being called to become the leader of the world.

This book is put together so it is easy to read. Each story is easy to relate to, each concept is easy to grasp. The difficulty will lie in your own ability to push the limits that you self-imposed on yourself such a long time ago and to facilitate the emergence of what is trying to make its way through your heart by way of everything that is going wrong in your life right now.

This book is a self-help guide toward success. As you know, success represents so many things to so many people. Your own definition of the word also evolves over time. When you think back, the way you would have described success, say, 10 years, 20 years, or 30 years ago is probably not the same as you would describe it today. Am I right?

Yes, of course your understanding of it changes along with your experiences, so naturally today you understand success in its current terms. I encourage you to follow the definition that you have of it right now, but with a certain degree of flexibility so it can bend, going backwards or forwards according to your circumstances. Think of it like bamboo: It doesn't break, just gets stronger and stronger after every storm. It will also grow with your achievements and soon enough you'll come to realize that, before achieving one more step toward success, your definition of it will have already changed, thereby preparing you for what is yet to unfold in your life.

Feel free to read one chapter at a time, or you can read the entire book in one afternoon. It's entirely up to you how you wish to use it, but you will undoubtedly end up reading it all!

Each chapter is designed in such a way that there is no specific order you need to follow when reading them. You can pick and choose whatever you need, you can follow your own intuition with regard to which part you want to start with. However, I just have one recommendation for you (not a requirement!): Complete the little exercises you find at the end of each chapter.

I know what you're thinking: "Oh, so I need to do some work too? I just wanted to read a good book!"

You will read a good book, I can promise you that, but what would be the point if it didn't start "rocking your world"?

Why read a book on self-help if it's not to help your own self?!

If you've been a "content collector" up until now, just imagine how different your life would have been by now if way back you had applied just one little piece of it? Don't let history repeat itself. Don't let your ego monopolize you into a forced status quo. Reclaim your liberty. Take control of your own freedom and make the decision that what matters most in life for you right now is YOU.

Dr. Michelle Nielsen

As an international speaker, healer, and writer, Dr. Michelle is a global leader in meditation and manifesting techniques. She specializes in "spiritual makeovers" and is the creator of *The Meditation Spa* **app**. Dr. Michelle enjoys a healthy, wellness lifestyle with her husband and two delightful children in Barcelona, Spain.

Facebook: https://www.facebook.com/MasterManifestors?fref=ts

Website: www.MasterManifestors.com

Free mini meditation e-course:

        http://mastermanifestors.com/one-win

TIP 1

The Secret Weapon of Ultra Successful Women

by Dr. Michelle Nielsen

Ladies, I am about to reveal the most powerful secret that you will ever discover on your journey toward professional and personal fulfillment. I have had the privilege of working in the wellness field and being intimately involved in the personal development movement for the past 20 years, and I can assure you that I have had access to some of the best teachers and techniques for success, health, and personal transformation available in the whole wide world.

I have both tried them all and prescribed them all.

However, I don't want you to have to spend the next 20 years digging around trying to discover this golden nugget. I would like to save you these 20 years of reading, travelling, and spending thousands of dollars on seminars by sharing with you a special insight into what I have learned. I also want to share with you what I believe is the most efficient, easy, enjoyable, and economical transformational tool on this planet.

What is this secret weapon that has been used for centuries by the most creative, intelligent and successful people in history?

It is a tool that will help lead you toward success in your finances, career, and all other aspects of your life. It will also help you achieve success in your health, relationships, and overall well-being.

This practice is not difficult, is not time consuming, and is certainly not expensive. However, it does require consistency and discipline.

That secret weapon is MEDITATION.

MEDITATION PUTS YOU IN THE DRIVER'S SEAT IN YOUR MIND AND IN YOUR LIFE.

So, what exactly is meditation?

Meditation is a practice whereby an individual trains his mind or induces a state of concentration, light trance, or higher consciousness either to realize some benefit or as an end in itself. Meditation can be used for deep relaxation, to bring about personal change, or to attain higher states of consciousness, creativity, and intelligence.

You see, we are all given an incredible piece of machinery that was designed to create an incredible life: the human brain. The human brain is the most powerful machine on the planet. It is more complex and efficient than the world's most powerful computer.

Did you know that even though it only weighs in at a mere three pounds (1.35 kg), the brain contains nearly 100 billion cells? Working, firing, and wiring together 24/7 to manage your body, your mind, your thoughts, and your life. From an energy point of view, it represents a very expensive piece of equipment for you to maintain. Scientists estimate that 20% to 25% of your total energy expenditure goes toward keeping your brain functioning!

Think of your brain as a powerful computer that stores your memory and controls how you, as a human, think and react. It has of course evolved over time and it features some incredibly intricate parts that scientists still struggle to understand today.

Unfortunately, our brain does not come with its own user manual; however, scientists are now starting to unravel the power of this amazing organ. As you know, most people are only using a small fraction (it's been estimated at about 10%) of their brain's total capacity. Or they are not using it effectively.

However, when we discover how to unleash the incredible power of our brain, we enter into the realm of genius. This is the realm where the ultra successful reside. And you'll soon get access to it as well.

Your powerful mind can be your biggest enemy or your most valuable asset. To quote from the world's oldest spiritual text, *The Bhagavad Gita:*

> *"The mind acts like an enemy for those who do not control it."*

Ultra successful people know how to master their mind.

Mastering your mind requires three essential elements:

1. Mental Purity:

When we are alert and rested in our mind, we have fresh ideas and are more productive. We are more likely to make better decisions. We have better problem-solving skills and we are more likely to produce new ideas.

When the brain is relaxed, our brain waves slow down into the alpha and theta states, thereby activating our right brain. This is where our creativity and genius lie. Meditation cleanses the mind. Think of it as a "mental shower": Even a short meditation session will flush out any negative emotions and thoughts that have been building up in our brain throughout the day. It's like pressing the reset button and starting afresh. Ultra successful women use meditation to rest, recharge, and reset their minds to enable them to take on any new challenges that arise while staying at the top of their game.

2. Mental Fitness (Flexibility & Strength):

Everyone faces challenges and obstacles throughout their lives and on their path to success. It's not what happens to us in life that determines the outcome, but rather how we respond to what happens to us— our knee-jerk emotional reaction to the challenges in life. When we take a moment to process these challenges and *choose* an appropriate response, we are more likely to make a wise decision. In the human brain, when we have stress and experience the emotion of fear, it sends out a massive amount of adrenaline, which is dumped into our system. This actually shuts down our logical thinking frontal lobe. Therefore, when fear rises, intelligence plummets. (Can you remember some of the worst decisions made in your life when you were in a highly emotional state?).

Emotional intelligence is when we allow ourselves to feel an emotion and then get to choose whether or not we want to process and respond to that emotion—or create a more proactive response. The quality of our life depends on the quality of our perspective. When we are open-minded and willing to put our ego to one side, we can change the way we look at our life's challenges. A small adjustment in perspective might give you the power to make a dramatic and positive change in your life's experiences.

3. Mental Discipline:

We are constantly bombarded with negative messages from the world. If we let these messages control and affect our own thoughts, then we are also letting the outside world control our thoughts. We end up having thoughts that are not ours. They are the thoughts of our culture, our society, and our environment. If you have any contact whatsoever with the daily news, Internet news, newspapers of any kind, or radio, you will be continually attacked with messages of negativity and fear. One would think that the world was always coming to an end! Unfortunately, disaster and bad news sells. Ultra successful people have learned to monitor, control, and choose their thoughts. They choose thoughts that support their visions and their dreams. They discard thoughts that are fear-based, negative, and unproductive. This makes them original thinkers, innovators, and leaders. Meditation is an effective practice to learn mental discipline.

It always amazes me how many people have discipline in so many areas of their lives (their diet, their fitness, and their schedule), yet so few people practice any form of mental discipline, which is what really directs the quality of our lives.

Control your thoughts, or your thoughts will control you!

The ultra-successful have mastered mental purity, mental fitness, and mental discipline. With patience and persistence, meditation is the tool that will help you master these areas as well.

Why is meditation so powerful?

Meditation helps you:

- Connect to your true genius
- Connect to your creative self
- Connect to your spiritual self
- Connect to the quantum field
- Master your right-brain/left-brain balance
- Combat the detrimental health effects of stress
- Keep in the flow

...and it is a feminine practice!

But you don't have to take my word for it. Many famous and successful people meditate. Maybe they will help you determine whether or not you can follow their path:

- Oprah Winfrey revealed in the media (actually she's revealed it many times) the profound effect meditation has had on her life. As she said: "The one thing I want to continue to do is to center myself every day and make that a practice for myself, because I am one thousand percent better when I do."
- Tina Turner (singer–songwriter, actress)
- Sheryl Crow (singer–songwriter)
- Madonna (singer–songwriter, actress)
- Paul McCartney (musician, The Beatles)
- Marshall McLuhan (educator, philosopher)
- Rupert Murdoch (media mogul)
- Gwyneth Paltrow (actress)
- Sting (singer, musician)
- The Dalai Lama (religious leader)

In addition:

- Albert Einstein (scientist)

- Mick Jagger (singer)
- Bruce Lee (martial arts expert)
- Jennifer Lopez (singer, actress)
- Clint Eastwood (actor, director, politician)
- Harrison Ford (actor)
- George Lucas (producer)
- Alice Walker (author)
- Jerry Seinfeld (comedian)
- William Ford Jr. (Ford Motor Company)

And:

- Richard Gere (actor)
- Tiger Woods (golf pro)
- Julia Roberts (actress)
- Goldie Hawn (actress)
- Oliver Stone (movie producer)
- Elle Macpherson (supermodel)
- Deepak Chopra (author)
- Wayne Dyer (author)

That is a pretty impressive list, by anyone's standards.

I do believe that the disconnection from inner strength and peace is what makes many of us sick, both emotionally and physically. Breathing and other forms of meditation, combined with other mind–body healing techniques are what I teach people in order to connect their spiritual self and discover their true power.

I also believe that the disconnection from the joy of knowing your true self is why many individuals get caught up in dangerous, unconstructive behaviors. Regular meditation helps you draw strength from your inner self, which is the true original source of inspiration, creativity, security, and joy. When we lose our connection with it, the void we feel is so painful that we will try anything to fill it.

25

In a desperate attempt to reclaim the "rush" of tapping into the power of their authentic selves, some people indulge in drugs and alcohol abuse, overeat or starve themselves, get involved in destructive relationships, overwork themselves at the office, or engage in extreme sports activities. If they would only slow down and take a moment to calm their minds, things would be very different.

In addition, through meditation, we slow our brain waves down into an alpha or theta state. It is in these states that I believe we are in connection with the "collective consciousness," as the famous psychologist Carl Jung spoke about. Modern physicists call this the "quantum field." It is the invisible energy that connects everything in existence. When we tap into this "field," we are on purpose and in flow, which is when we experience those wonderful synchronicities and inspired coincidences that help usher our dreams into reality.

Hopefully, by now, you can understand why I am so passionate about and in love with meditation.

In conclusion, I would like to say to all you wonderful women reading this chapter that meditation is a feminine practice. With meditation we stay connected to our true inner self. We nurture our soul. Through meditation, we take a break from the masculine attributes of success (ego, striving, drive, pushing ourselves, competitiveness). When we distance ourselves from these things, we are more likely to pursue a more feminine model of success that keeps us in flow, creative, and graceful. Through meditation, we are connected with our true Goddess, who will usher us toward the life we dream of and deserve.

Here is a little exercise to help you get started:

ADDING BREATHING MEDITATION TO YOUR WELLNESS ROUTINE:

Although there are hundreds of effective meditation techniques, I would like to introduce you to a simple meditation technique called "breathing meditation."

The advantage of breathing meditation is that it is easy to do at any time and anywhere, not only at home. You can do breathing meditation in groups or on the sly, quite incognito and unrecognizable, as it looks very much like a nap from the "outside in." Unlike chanting meditation, for example, disturbing other people is not an issue as breathing meditation makes absolutely no sound.

Steps in a 10–15 minute breathing meditation

Step 1: Set your timer for 10 to 15 minutes.

Step 2: Get comfortable and breathe. Wherever you're meditating, allow your body to relax and take your first few cleansing breaths.

Step 3: Keep breathing. Slowly allow your body to breathe normally, in and out, through your nose. Concentrate on the air flowing in and out of your body. Feel it rush through your nose and fill your lungs.

Step 4: Get and stay focused. Focus all of your attention on your breathing, relaxing every time you feel your muscles beginning to tense. Pay particular attention to the sensation of the breath flowing in and out of your nose. When your attention wanders, as it most likely will, simply notice what is happening and return your focus to the air flowing in and out of your body.

Initially you might spend most—or even all—of your time re-directing your attention to your breathing. Do not be discouraged. This is a natural part of the practice, a wonderful experience of observing your thoughts and feelings through the eyes of your true self, your spirit.

Continue until you hear the sound of your timer.

Through this and all meditation practices, you will be able to connect with your Goddess and become who you really are, more and more, every day.

I wish you good luck with your breathing meditation practice. For the next 30 days, try to incorporate it into your life twice a day, every day, as this is the way to master meditation and make it a daily habit for your success and well-being.

If you would like to explore additional meditation techniques, I encourage you to sign up for my free meditation course, which I created. This is available at http://mastermanifestors.com/one-win or within my The Meditation Spa app.

Faith J. Dugan

Faith Dugan, M.P.A., has more than 20 years of accounting experience in the private, non-profit, and government sectors, managing multi-million dollar budgets. She holds a bachelor's degree in accounting and management as well as a master's degree in public administration. She teaches money mastery techniques, sets up financial structures, and helps free women from bondage beliefs, keeping them a slave to money on a mission to create money mastery mamas.

Website:	http://www.askthemoneymentor.com
Website:	http://moneymasterymama.com
Facebook:	https://www.facebook.com/faithjdugan
Facebook:	https://www.facebook.com/themoneymentor
Twitter:	https://twitter.com/askmoneymentor
LinkedIn:	http://www.linkedin.com/in/faithduganmpa
Pinterest:	http://pinterest.com/themoneymentor

TIP 2

Be a Money Mastery Mama

by Faith J. Dugan

Have you ever felt like a slave to money? Do you find money intimidating or shameful? Do you feel like you are bad at math or believe women are just not good at math? Do you feel guilty negotiating or asking for a raise? Do you feel guilty about making more money than your husband or significant other? Women have made so much progress the last few decades, so why are so many still struggling with money and many times refusing to act in their own financial best interest? It is my deepest desire to empower women and shed these barriers that are keeping you hostage.

Why should you strive to be a money mastery mama? First of all, limiting your financial abundance and mastery is keeping yourself small and what you offer to the world. Second, money problems can spill over to your relationships, affect your health, and cloud your happiness. Finally, if you do not fix your relationship with money, what kind of example are you setting for your children? Are you a good role model to them?

MY STORY

I understand being scared of money. Growing up, I was never taught anything about money from my parents or school. My mother, being raised during the Great Depression, had a dysfunctional relationship with strong limiting beliefs about money.

I was in a controlling, abusive marriage with a husband who had a dysfunctional relationship with money, leading to constant worries about bills and utilities being shut off. I finally left without a dime to my name, not knowing how I would support myself and my twin five-year-old boys, as I had no job skills and no money. I didn't have a clue how I was going to make it; I was scared out of my mind.

Not only did I succeed, I persevered and have made it my life's purpose to learn everything I can about money so I can empower women to be money masters.

MONEY BLOCKS

Fear, confusion, and guilt are the primary emotions keeping women from mastering their money. Fear and confusion cause women to avoid dealing with their finances. They might think it's a man's job and rely on their husband to manage the finances until something tragic like a divorce or sudden death occurs, when the wife is suddenly overwhelmed with the responsibility of managing her finances on her own. Now what?

Avoidance creates more chaos, like unnecessary late fees, fines, and penalties. If they aren't looking at their bills, revenue issues or billing errors go unnoticed. Not filing taxes on time or keeping up on bookkeeping, disorganization, and losing important receipts are very costly. If, during an audit, receipts are illegible or not found, they must pay penalties, which could've been avoided. Credit card companies love people who aren't paying attention so they can charge high fees and interest rates. Money mastery includes learning to master your credit cards to improve your credit so you can use them in your favor, leveraging them to make money rather than lose it.

Many people buy things to feel better and raise their self-esteem or impress others. Spending above your means is a surefire plan to failure. Your financial situation is a direct reflection of your inner relationship with money.

Guilt can lead many moms to indulge their children with money, especially if there has been a divorce or lost spouse. This does not teach kids the skills for money mastery; rather, it teaches them that making mom feel guilty gets them whatever they want, setting them up for a dysfunctional relationship with money.

STEPS YOU CAN TAKE TO BE A MONEY MASTERY MAMA

Invest in yourself first. Take care of yourself first, or you won't have anything to give others. Many women are taught to be martyrs and put themselves last. You cannot help your child if you are not taking care of yourself. In order for your child to have self-esteem, you must model it first. You cannot give to others what you don't have in yourself.

Education. Make a priority of educating yourself about your finances. Hire a coach or take classes. These will save you time, stress, money, fines, penalties, and credit dings. You can't change what you don't understand. Paying attention to your money will attract and grow wealth.

Organization. You can't change what you don't acknowledge, so organizing your finances is critical. A messy desk piled with paperwork leaves you feeling disorganized, overwhelmed, and drained. Organization creates a positive energy in your office and mind.

Support and Delegation. Women can be really bad at asking for help, wanting to be superwomen who do it all. Successful entrepreneurs don't do everything on their own, especially with tasks that are draining and outside their expertise. Enlisting support allows you to feel more joy doing what you love best, and money loves joy!

Gratefulness. Do you dread paying bills or taxes? Being in that energy disallows money from flowing into your life, creating the opposite of what you want. Think of ALL the things you have to be grateful for. Gratitude allows money to flow in. Be thankful for being able to pay the bills, thankful you can buy food, thankful you have money to buy clothes, shelter, or heat. Be thankful you have to pay taxes because you make a good income. My tip for shifting from dread to gratefulness is to write "thank you" on the memo of a check. Make paying bills fun! That joy removes negative low vibrational feelings like guilt, envy, depression, and fear, which block wealth abundance.

Generosity. Hoarding is a scarcity mindset. As you become more generous, giving from a state of joy, not obligation, you will attract money in your life. Money is energy; it's about giving *and* receiving. In order to become wealthy, you must enjoy releasing money.

Affirmations. Change your inner dialogue about money to change your money story. One way to do this is to write a list of money affirmations that resonate with you, reciting them in front of a mirror twice a day for maximum effectiveness.

Examples:

"Money comes to me easily and effortlessly."

"I love creating wealth."

"I always spend money wisely."

"I always have enough money for my needs."

"Financial success is mine."

Be a Money Mastery Mama! One of the best ways to improve your money IQ is by teaching your kids about money mastery. Play money games with your children to make learning fun, set them up with a healthy relationship with money, improve their confidence, and release any fears surrounding it.

EXERCISE: TEACH YOUR KIDS MONEY MASTERY:

1. **Make your kids responsible for expenditures outside the basic necessities you provide.** Do they want the latest album by their favorite band? Now they have the power to pay for it with their own money. Deciding whether or not they want a nice shirt for $10 or a designer shirt for $50 is a powerful lesson; it teaches financial responsibility while encouraging gratefulness for what they have. Where does this money come from? Well, you're going to…

2. **Pay them weekly "wages" for tasks outside their normal chores.** Because you are now only paying for their basic necessities, you've moved the money you were already spending on them to their wages, which is tied to their extra chores.

3. **They are responsible for weekly "family fun" taxes.** Everyone contributes to a family activity set at least once per month. Alternatively, this could also be used to contribute to charity as a "tax write-off" if you want to reward them with a family activity yourself.

4. **Go over their financial report monthly.** How much are they saving and spending? If they've set a goal to buy something in the future, like a car, how much closer are they to that goal? Should they adjust their saving/spending? This is also a good time to decide the next "family fun tax" activity.

5. **Have them write their own money affirmations.** Developing a positive relationship with money at an early age is critical.

6. **Sign them up with a credit union and a credit card.** At a certain age they might be eligible for a low-limit or secured card; don't pass up this opportunity to teach your child! Alternatively, you can add them as an authorized account to your own unused low-limit credit card. You can also sign them up for a credit union savings and checking account (some offer credit cards); now their savings can garner interest. Most credit unions specialize in car loans, which is helpful for teenagers ready to buy their first car. Building a positive credit history ensures that your child won't be saddled with bad loans and credit rates as they enter adulthood.

Ironically, many women tend to focus much of their attention on their relationships, yet neglect their relationship with money. You can change this! I have only begun to scratch the surface of money mastery in this chapter. I encourage you to take these first few baby steps. Everybody wins when you are financially empowered, especially your children. Becoming a money mastery role model will inspire your children by giving them the tools and knowledge to set them up for financial success. How wonderful would that be?

Dona Davis

Dona Davis is a certified special education teacher and certified life coach. She taught school for over 35 years and coaches not only employment seekers, but also individuals and groups who are transitioning from one point to another in their lives. Dona empowers women to their full potential by creating a safe space for them to slowly transition from where they are to where they want to be.

Website:	http://www.coachdona.com
Facebook:	http://www.facebook.com/tipsfromyourjobcoach
Pinterest:	http://pinterest.com/donamdavis/boards/
LinkedIn:	http://www.linkedin.com/profile/ view?id=66195574&trk=nav_responsive_tab_profile

TIP 3

8 Strategies for a Successful Search for Employment

by Dona Davis

With so many people competing for employment positions in this bleak economy, the competition is fierce! I offer a few strategies to assist you with your search for employment. The old school ways of finding work are a bit outdated. You have to mix the old methods with the new methods. Here's how to develop your strategic plan:

1. **Network:** Networking is your first step for letting others know what you need. You should be specific. Tell them your talent and what position you are looking for.

2. **Research:** Research the company you want to work for. Learn what the climate is there, the corporate environment, and the attitude of the people who work there. This will help you decide if you really want to work there. A company might look good on the outside, but the inside might be something else entirely.

3. **More research:** Look at the job description. Find the keywords used to describe their needs. Use these keywords in both your resume and cover letter. This is how you optimize your resume. Keywords are buzz words, and when you submit your resume

full of buzz words, their computer will notice. This puts you on the top of the pile and in front of your competition.

4. **The Internet:** Use search engines to find vacant positions in your local area. In the search bar, enter the position you want and your city and state. You'll be amazed at what pops up!

5. **Use the Yellow Pages:** In many instances, the classified section of the newspaper is irrelevant. Consider using the Yellow Pages telephone directory to find work. Why not? It's how I found my very first professional position. The Yellow Pages telephone directory gives information about businesses in your community. Select employers based on your areas of interest. Just look up a topic of interest, look below the heading to find companies you would like to work for, and contact them directly.

6. **Information Interview:** An information interview is when you call a prospective employer and ask to come in for a tour of their business. Why? You get to take a look around and ask questions. You get to check out their operation, their climate, and their culture. These are the things you want to know about to determine if it's a good fit for you. You are in charge. You ask all the questions, so make sure you have at least 5 good ones. Leave your resume at home, but take your business card with your contact information. While you're there, solve one of their problems for them. This evokes curiosity about you.

7. **Your Employment Interview:** There are 4 common types of employment interviews: telephone, behavioral, situational, and informational. Oftentimes these interviews take place in one meeting. The telephone interview begins when the prospective employer calls to inquire more information about you. This is a much different information interview than previously discussed. They might need clarification about something you filled out on your employment application or more contact information from a reference you provided. The behavioral interview is the most commonly practiced. You will be asked questions to determine how you handled or will handle something. The situational interview determines how you will handle a specific situation that has occurred or might occur.

Make sure you ask questions when your interviewer asks "Do you have any questions for me?" Be sure to have at least 5 good questions ready. You will formulate your questions as you conduct your research. If not, then you need to go back and research more thoroughly. Keep in mind that, when you ask questions, the interview turns into a conversation. Remember that you have a certain amount of control during your employment interview. You never want to seem uninterested or bored. The interviewer is taking notes. You should take notes during your interview. Jot down a few questions yourself. Solve a problem for them right then and there during your interview. Demonstrate your competency right then and there. This will pique their interest even further, and your name will wind up in the top 10! A good interview takes about 20 minutes. If your interview is less than 20 minutes, you are not a good contender. Be sure to write a "thank you letter" for both the interviewer and the gatekeeper. Do this immediately after your interview—it does count.

Beware of illegal interview questions. You do not have to answer them, and the interviewer knows it. It's not likely you will be asked one; however, one might come up during your interview depending on how much personal information you share during your pre-interview. Be mindful of how you conduct yourself in the lobby and in the reception area. That's where the gatekeeper is, and it's their job to inform the interviewer. Avoid using your cell phone in the reception area.

8. **Volunteer:** Why on earth would you want to do that? Volunteering at a company has advantages. After you call and ask for an information interview, you can volunteer your services for a specific period of time. You can also ask for reference letters before your volunteer period ends. This is valuable because after your volunteering you have at least one contact there, the company knows your work ethic, you can legitimately ask them for references. You will be familiar with them and they with you based on the experience you gained.

During your employment interview, always keep the potential employer's best interests in mind. They are focused on their core mission. Ask questions related to how you can move the company forward. Prove to them that you are indeed the best candidate for the job. Your search for employment is ongoing. Keep abreast of the newest trends, and be flexible and creative in your search.

Kate Gardner

Kate Gardner is an international life coach, author, and motivational speaker. Kate informs, motivates, and empowers women to help them uncover their purpose in life. Kate helps clients see their value in the world and teaches them how to package their purpose and sell it to the world. She is also the CEO and founder of the global The Freedom & Empowerment Campaign. Kate inspires by sharing her story with the world.

Website: www.katygardner.com
Website: www.survivor-to-thriver.com
Campaign Website: www.freedomandempowerment.com
Email: Kate@survivor-to-thriver.com
Twitter: www.twitter.com/kategardner1979
Facebook Page: www.facebook.com/
                       freedomandempowermentcampaign
Facebook Profile: www.facebook.com/kit1979

TIP 4

Survivor to Thriver

by Kate Gardner

The data indicates that 1 in 3 women and 1 in 6 men now suffer some form of domestic violence within their lifetime. This means that, while you are sitting here reading this, 1.6 billion people on this planet are suffering daily. We live in a society that chooses to ignore this major global issue, as if it is just an issue in relationships that should be kept behind closed doors. In reality, this is something the world seriously needs to be educated on so that deaths don't occur each week and the 750,000 children who witness domestic violence each year don't grow up suffering with emotional and mental health issues.

Why am I so passionate about this issue?

I was one of those women that experienced child sex abuse and abusive relationships. I was completely groomed for failure as a child and witnessed and experienced many things a child shouldn't. When a child is not educated in how life should be, the conditions and surroundings in which they live shape their mindset and they think that the life they experience is normal. As a result, they grow up not expecting anything better. My childhood had set the foundations for me to have one abusive relationship after another. I felt like a complete failure and had very little confidence, and my expectations of life were not very high.

By the age of 19 I had two children of my own, but the relationship with my children's father didn't last. We were far too young, and the pressure of children didn't help our relationship to succeed. So I began the journey alone as a single parent.

At the age of 22 I began working in a food factory. Three months into my employment, I had an affair with my married boss. The relationship was based on psychological abuse, and the mental scars that I endured from that relationship caused me to drink. I suffered from depression, which drove me to attempt suicide by slitting my wrists with a kitchen knife. Just as I began to cut into my right wrist, the father of my children broke through my kitchen window to stop me.

The tables turned in the next relationship I had at the age of 25. I had now become the abuser. I ruined a 5-year relationship with my drinking and constant paranoia. The deeply hurt child within me had surfaced and was lashing out.

By the age of 28 I was a professional woman with a successful business and had the world at my feet—or so it seemed. In reality, I was an overweight alcoholic who took drugs each weekend to escape the reality of my depression and mental scars. This all became a harsh reality one day when I was unable to climb the stairs without becoming breathless. So I took up running, and the extra weight dropped in no time. My head cleared, and I stopped drinking and quit smoking and never touched drugs again. I couldn't repair the relationship I was in at the time because I had damaged it too much. I was now also starting to become a new person.

I went to stay with a friend for a weekend and was delighted to see someone I had not seen for 10 years. That night he told me I was beautiful and that he would give me an amazing life and make me really happy. So we began a relationship and, after about 4 months of seeing him, I was groomed and blinded by love so much that I asked him to move in with me and my children. We moved 6 miles away to the countryside and planned our wedding.

After 4 months of living in utter bliss, he started to drink heavily, which resulted in frequent arguments in which he often accused me of sleeping with everyone. Each evening would end the same, with him rolling in from the pub, drunk, and sitting on the end of the bed to wake me and torture me with accusations. Most of the time he would wake my children too.

Not long after, the psychological abuse began. He locked me in the house one evening and wouldn't let me go. I tried to escape only to have my legs trapped in the door; he slammed the door on my legs 3 more times so that I couldn't walk. I eventually made my escape through the kitchen window when he needed to use the bathroom. Unfortunately, I only made it to the bottom of the road before he caught up with me. He pried my mobile phone out of my hands and punched me in the face. I fell to the ground, completely shocked that the man I was due to marry in 6 weeks had battered me at the roadside. He started walking back toward the house, shouting back over his shoulder that I had "best find a park bench to sleep on because I was not coming back in the house."

I scraped myself up off the road and limped to the nearest public phone, where I called the police and reported him for assault. But I felt soft the morning after and continued to put up with his abuse for another 3 weeks until my body gave in with the stress and I suffered a stroke, leaving me paralyzed down the right side of my body. Lying in the hospital bed with a limp body and a stutter as the right side of my brain was not functioning properly was the major wake-up call I needed to leave him.

A week into my recovery I threw him out of the house. I cancelled the wedding and found a new home for me and my children to start a new life. He continued to stalk me afterwards and even broke through my kitchen window and stood over me in my bed one evening just to make sure I was not dating anyone new. Finally, after several warnings from the police, he left town and my children and I started to rebuild our lives. My body was getting stronger by the day, and I learned to smile again.

Until I received a phone call that pulled the rug from underneath me once more: My daughter had been raped.

Why us? What the hell had I done to deserve all this pain? I sat on the edge of my bed one evening staring at the wall. My only intention was to drink to numb the pain, but I had done so well not to for 4 years.

I didn't want to go backwards with my life. So I stood up to unpack boxes to keep my mind occupied.

Staring at me from the bottom of one box was the book that completely changed my life: *The Secret*, by Rhonda Byrnes. I learned about the film that had been made from the book, which ultimately led me to my first mentor, Jack Canfields, who taught me about the rule of 5.

The meaning of the rule of 5 is that you complete 5 goals per day to reach the big picture you have set in your mind. So take a huge goal and break it down into 5 smaller steps per day, then each week you increase these goals to become bigger and better than the week before.

My first huge goal was to overcome domestic violence, which I did using this rule. Eighteen months ago, my rule of 5 looked something like this:

1. Get out of bed
2. Clean the house
3. Go to work
4. Make dinner and sit down with the children
5. Go to bed

Today my rule of 5 looks more like this:

1. Start the morning with a 9-mile run
2. Coach clients
3. Complete a media interview or meeting
4. Work with my team of 21 people to create something amazing for victims of abuse
5. Write my chapter for an international bestselling book

The rule of 5 helped me become an international author/life coach/ speaker and founder of the global charity called The Freedom & Empowerment Campaign, which is known in 17 countries and holds a team of 21 people from across 7 countries who are all bestselling authors and speakers.

And my daughter? Emily is the co-founder of The Freedom & Empowerment Teen Campaign, which educates teens on dating violence. She too has her own ambassadors, who are also bestselling authors and speakers.

I urge you to use this rule of 5 to help you draw closer to those big goals you have envisioned, because hitting concrete bottom only gives you the foundations to re-build your life.

Amanda Sue Howell

Amanda Sue is a visionary, a creator, and a muncher of sour candies. She likes her photography macro, her chocolate dark, and her soda in garish bright green. She's the mother of four amazing children and the wife of a fellow veteran of the United States Air Force. Her multiple passions include coaching quirky creatives, correcting grammar, learning new crafts, photographing the world around her, singing, and of course being with her family. She also hates talking in the third person.

Website: www.amandasuehowell.com
Facebook: www.facebook.com/amandsuehowell
Twitter: @amandsuehowell
Pinterest: www.pinterest.com/amandsuehowell
Instagram: amandasuehowell

Quirky, Creative, and Uniquely You

by Amanda Sue Howell

I've never been trendy.

I've never been popular.

I've never been a cheerleader, or a magician, or a spelling bee champion. Nothing about me is remarkable—at least not on the surface.

Despite my seeming unremarkable, people remember me. I've attended events and years later, musicians from the event remember meeting me. Actually, embarrassingly enough, I can name at least one occasion when they remembered meeting me and I didn't remember meeting them!

I don't say this to brag, but to make my point. I have no mystique. I have no bizarre facial features that make me stand out. So why am I memorable? I believe it's for one simple reason: I am me. Through and through, for better or worse, I am 100% myself.

I come from a family of memorable women. My mom is a redhead and one of the most level-headed, laidback people you'll ever meet (contrarily enough, I'm not a redhead, but I got the temper!). She's also the homeschooling teacher of all 10 of her children (yes, that included me). My grandmother was also quite a force to be reckoned with. She was a teacher, a volunteer in her church, and a missionary in Mexico for a time.

Not only have I never been trendy, but I tend to consciously buck whatever the trend is. I don't want to "fit in," I was made to stand out! My hair has been numerous colors, including ones not found in hair's natural spectrum. I've worn corsets as everyday wear. I've had 7 piercings and would have had more, except I had to remove them when I was in basic military training.

I take honesty seriously and will tell the truth about myself, even to my detriment. I have teeth that the vampire crowd goes crazy over, but I was made fun of for them when I was a kid. I've had a haircut that went so horribly wrong that I looked like my brother. I'm extremely passionate, which means I love with all my heart. It also means that when I'm angry, it's like a wildfire sweeping through. It's over fast, but boy is it intense!

But all of these things—the good and the bad—are me. Thank God I married a man who doesn't love me despite these things, but because of them. Everything has its reasons.

Yes, a woman with a redhead's temper can be a force of nature, but if I were less passionate, I wouldn't be as devoted to the causes that break my heart. The same fiery passion that makes me defend my stance to the very end is the very same passion that makes me wildly empathetic.

All of this uniqueness can (and should) apply to your business. What sets you apart, what makes you memorable, is what will bring clients to you (and back to you!). You know your stuff; your photography has the angels weeping for joy, you can write words that will live on for years to come, but what makes you different from the other amazing entrepreneurs? How do you make your business truly stand out?

It boils down to 3 C's: color, copywriting, and content. Each of these is a piece of the puzzle that forms a "Uniquely You" website. Let me explain each in a bit more detail, and then I'll give you some action steps to put into practice with your business.

Color

You can't visit Sandi Krakowski's site without realizing that she loves hot pink. The arrow in her call to action is hot pink. Her "get your attention font" is hot pink. She even has a hot pink streak in her hair!

Color is part of telling a story. It creates emotion, feeds the senses, and adds detail. Even different shades of the same color can have different connotations. I feel very differently seeing hot pink than I do seeing baby pink. And don't get me started on stomach medicine pink. Twitter and Facebook both use blue for their logo, but they use very different shades of blue.

Questions to get you started:

- What's your favorite color?
- What colors do you like to wear?
- What color is your phone case, or your purse, or your favorite snuggly throw?
- What flowers make you smile?
- What colors are evoked by your favorite season?

Tip: Don't be scared if you like colors that someone else already uses. As I mentioned earlier, Twitter and Facebook both use blue, but no one would ever confuse those two websites. My friend Prerna Malik and I both have had orange and blue on our sites, but our websites have very different feelings to them.

Copywriting

We all have a different voice. Even if we have similar content, the way we write it will come across differently, especially when you learn to write the way you talk. Let's use cooking shows as an example. Choose any two cooking shows, and odds are they have completely different styles. One might have a down home country feel whereas the other might have that rock and roll edge.

The French *"je ne sais quoi"* literally means "I don't know what." When I was younger, I ran across the term in a book and asked my dad what it meant. He defined it as "that certain something." It might not be the literal translation, but it works beautifully. The *je ne sais quoi*, in terms of your website, is that undefinable pizzazz that sets you apart.

The truly wonderful websites have that *je ne sais quoi*. They've got a biting sarcasm or hilarious wit or profound insight. It's the website that you come back to over and over again, not because you need to, but because you want to. It's that thing you're drawn to, even if you could never explain why.

Questions to get you started:

- Is there something unique about your speaking style? Do you pause like William Shatner? Do you throw in words from non-English languages? Do you speak very properly?

- Do you bring pop culture references into your speech? Do you have a favorite actor you quote a lot? Do you adore the works of Jane Austen and reference them?

- What are your favorite books to read? Movies to watch? Songs to listen to?

- What are your favorite websites to read? What pulls you in? Wit? Knowledge? Amazing photography? (Remember that pictures can speak volumes as well.)

Tip: Don't be afraid to bring these things into your site copy, where it's appropriate, but make sure you're respecting copyright and fair use laws.

Content

Once you've determined colors and you've established your voice, the final piece is your content. Think of it like a book. The colors are the cover of the book, the pictures, and everything that gives a book its aesthetic appeal. Your voice or copywriting style is the genre of the book. Is it a fairy tale? Is it a documentary? Is it a biography? The content is the actual story. What is your story?

Your story is your why. It's the beat to your song. It's what makes a business *your* business. It's the final thing that sets your website and your business apart. Your story goes into your "about" page and your "why work with me" page. It's the hidden background for everything you do.

I love quotes. All kinds of quotes: quirky quotes, quotes filled with wisdom, and quotes from books. One of my current favorites is from a TED presentation I watched. It's from a man named Simon Sinek, who said, "People don't buy what you do. They buy why you do it." I wrote that quote down on a sticky note and posted it on my wall above my desk. I looked at it the entire time I did my last site makeover. It was the driving thought behind rewriting my copy, and it even helped me re-do my tagline. I wanted to make sure that my target market knows they're home the minute they lay eyes on my site.

Questions to get you started:

- Why did you start this business?
- What is your driving force?
- What causes the tug at your heart?

Tip: Sometimes the very things that drive you become the reasons for your business. Erin Giles is an amazing example of this. She started off with a pretty standard coaching business, but one day her eyes were opened to the human trafficking industry. She now runs a thriving business teaching entrepreneurs to tie their businesses to the causes that tug at their heartstrings, thereby creating a movement.

Putting it All Together

Okay, now it's time for you to create your own unique concept. Write down the answers to the questions and look at them. Do they create a cohesive theme? Where can you make adjustments?

Once you've figured out color, copy, and content that meld together nicely, you'll have a better idea of where to put the unique touches that will transform a business into *your* business. The world is waiting for your unique qualities, so get out there and rock!

Kim Boudreau Smith

Kim Boudreau Smith is creator of Power UP Inside/OUT, international business consultant, strategist and coach, speaker, international bestselling author and radio show host. Kim mentors women to strengthen their business to become top producers in their lives. Kim teaches other women to sell like a Woman! Kim is a direct, no-nonsense cheerleader for her clients, supporting them to live the dream of their lives. Kim also owns a fitness business.

Website:	www.kimbsmith.com
Website:	http://www.blogtalkradio.com/leadherupisin
Facebook:	https://www.facebook.com/kboudreausmith
Facebook:	https://www.facebook.com/KimBoudreauSmith
Twitter:	https://twitter.com/KimBSmithInc
LinkedIn:	http://www.linkedin.com/in/kimboudreausmith

TIP 6

Super Woman Syndrome: Not Losing Yourself

by Kim Boudreau Smith

The song that was used in a famous perfume commercial back in the early 1980s (yes, I just dated myself!) suggests that we are superwomen and can do it all; well we can, but what is our all? Even today, women all over the world are still running an enormous risk of endangering themselves mentally, spiritually, physically, and emotionally because of the Superwoman Syndrome. On top of raising families, more women today are also becoming entrepreneurs and major financial contributors to their families. How do we do both without losing our minds, health, and spirituality? We *can* have it all without losing ourselves.

The work I do with my female clients always begins with an understanding of their life purpose: children, spouses/partners, business, and all of the decisions relating to each. Only then can we venture into learning how to sell ourselves as women entrepreneurs. This information could fill an entire book, but we're going to concisely encapsulate it here.

Ladies, take a look at successful companies; they all have well-defined purpose statements and core values. Take a minute to consider whether or not you have defined a personal purpose statement. Even family units should have purpose statements. However, this chapter will focus on businesswomen who are doing it all without compromising their overall well-being.

The purpose statement, like a map, provides a clear direction and reminds you of your desired destination: what your passion is and why you are truly here. Your purpose statement will keep you on track and guide you when to say "yes" and when to say "no." That's right— the word "no" needs to be a part of our vocabulary!

So let's begin.

Getting off the treadmill. To begin living a more focused and less chaotic life, consider the following 12 steps:

Step 1: Start with a life purpose statement.

Step 2: Expand that statement with everything you do that is vital to your life's purpose.

Step 3: List areas of your life that you do not need to be doing. These are your no's.

Step 4: List your must do's: What roles must you be doing?

Step 5: Begin a new game plan.

Step 6: Consider yourself to be your own best friend.

Step 7: Gather your village or community of support.

Step 8: Look out for time wasters and eliminate them.

Step 9: Learn to say no, and do this often without the estrogen guilt.

Step 10: Delegate, delegate, delegate. Do not be afraid to let go.

Step 11: Reward yourself for accomplishments and changes.

Step 12: Be crystal clear on what your needs are. Don't complicate your life by reaching for the shiny objects otherwise known as distractions.

These are basic, simple steps to start working toward a phenomenal life. There really is no specific order with the exception of Step 1: You must begin with your life purpose as your foundation.

As women we feel that we can do it all and, quite frankly, we can! However, if we show up depleted at the end of the day, we need to find balance. When we are completely clear on our life's purpose, then we can find that balance as we raise families and grow businesses. Clarity on what we answer "yes" or "no" to comes easier. When you know your purpose and direction, the guilt of saying no to things that don't fit goes away.

We can be superwomen without losing ourselves, especially when Superwoman knows in which direction she is flying. Once we have a clear direction, it's all about implementing plans and goals, becoming and staying organized, stopping the endless treadmill, and taking back control for managing our lives.

I know my purpose. Now what? After writing your life purpose statement, ask yourself a few more questions to determine your next steps:

> **What are you currently doing that is leading toward fulfilling your purpose?**
>
> _____
> _____
> _____
> _____
> _____
> _____
> _____
>
> **What are you doing (or tolerating) that is not essential to your life's purpose?**
>
> _____
> _____
> _____
> _____
> _____
> _____
> _____

What obstacles have hindered you to date in fulfilling your life's purpose?

_____

_____

_____

_____

_____

_____

_____

What do you have to do differently (or give up) to fulfill your life's purpose?

_____

_____

_____

_____

_____

_____

How will you make this happen? What will it take?

_____

_____

_____

_____

_____

_____

Share with yourself how it feels to be Superwoman:

_____

_____

_____

_____

_____

_____

Check off any of the following that apply to you:

( ) I say *yes* to most people/requests

( ) I become anxious when I must say *no*

( ) I am consistently overwhelmed

( ) I constantly feel I'm not accomplishing enough

( ) At times I am anxious when I go to bed

( ) I run from one task to the next

( ) I do not schedule time for myself

( ) I continue to add more to my plate

( ) I feel like I'm stuck on a treadmill and can't get off

( ) I am overly stressed

If you checked off any of the above, you are running the risk of Superwoman Syndrome—trying to do it all and losing yourself. This is so unhealthy and needs to change now.

Helpful hints to handle your day: Remember that you must have your life's purpose completed before moving forward. These simple suggestions can then guide you to fulfillment:

1. Get up earlier to allow quiet and private time for you.
2. Learn to pay less attention to time—do not be a clock watcher. This distraction can lead us into the paradox of feeling we do not have enough time to do it all.
3. Regulate how many items you put on your "to do" list.
4. During lunch, avoid talking or doing anything business related. Whether you work from home or an office, do not eat lunch at your desk.
5. Surround yourself with enthusiastic and positive like-minded individuals.
6. Schedule daily breaks for yourself.

7. Be willing to say *no*. It's okay for *no* to be a part of our vocabulary.

8. Don't be afraid to ask for help when necessary.

9. Delegate what you can.

10. Have your "I am" positive affirmation statements on Post-it notes to support yourself in the changes you are implementing.

11. When you feel depressed, start a gratitude journal or list of things that you are grateful for.

12. Learn to relax. Try meditation, a walk outside, yoga, exercising, etc.

13. Pay attention to your inner self; listen to your needs.

14. End your day on a positive note, acknowledging successes.

15. Most of all, have fun and keep everything as simple as humanly possible!

Many talented, creative, and passionate women have stepped unwittingly into the role of Superwoman. They have donned the cape and mask and hindered their chances for success and balance.

Because you have chosen to put on the Superwoman costume, you can also make the choice to take it off. By removing the costume, you have the potential and ability to become a woman who is less stressed and more open to simply doing the best that you can without the compulsive need to be perfect. This is what I call having it all without losing yourself.

You will receive so many benefits from stepping off the treadmill and enjoying life without having to do it all. Throw away that Superwoman costume and only say *yes* to those activities that support your life's purpose.

You can have it all as long as you are clear and stay true to your life's purpose

Terry Wildemann

For intuitive business alchemist and success coach Terry Wildemann, studying and understanding how to achieve success in business and life has been a passion and lifelong quest. She merges her extensive business experience with her holistic and Law of Attraction knowledge in her speaking, coaching, and professional development workshops to help entrepreneurs and professionals transform their businesses and lives. Terry's weekly Blog Talk Radio show, "Coffee With Terry: Where Business and Spirituality Meet," offers business building wisdom from both Terry and her guests. Listen in and join in the conversation at www.coffeewithterry.com. Even better, apply to be a guest!

Website:	www.HeartCenteredSuccess.com
	www.CoffeeWithTerry.com
Facebook:	http://Facebook.com/TerryWildemann
	http://Facebook.com/HeartCenteredSuccess
	http://Facebook.com/CoffeeWithTerry
	http://Facebook.com/CallofTheRose
Twitter:	http://Twitter.com/TerryWildemann
	http://Twitter.com/CoffeeWithTerry
	http://Twitter.com/CallofTheRose
Pinterest:	http://Pinterest.com/TerryWildemann
LinkedIn:	http://LinkedIn.com/in/TerryWildemann

TIP 7

Burned Out? Re-Ignite Your life Like a Hot Mama!

by Terry Wildemann, CEC, CPCC

Ana-Do-It-All loved being busy and caring. She always had something to do and someone to care for, and when asked to do more, she always said "yes!" Her go, go, go attitude toward school, her career and business, and her family helped her do so much for others, but when it came time to care for herself, she always said "No, I'll take care of me later."

Unfortunately, Ana-Do-It-All's body kept giving her hints about caring for herself, but she didn't listen. Helping others, getting the job done right, and making people happy were so much more important! Finally, after her body gave out for the sixth time, taking weeks to recover each time, Ana-Do-It-All decided to get to the root of the burnout and discover how to avoid it in the future. She wanted answers as to why the burnout kept happening and what she needed to do to stop it. After all, it wasn't just her body that suffered. Her family, friends, and clients suffered with her.

There's a saying: "When the student is ready the teacher will come." Ana-Do-It-All was ready to listen and learn.

And the Journey Begins

While sitting in a nice comfy chair in her office, Ana-Do-It-All was pondering where to go for help. She was a leader, and in the back of her mind she was thinking of all the folks in her life who would benefit from what she would learn about stopping the behavior and re-igniting her life.

Something made her look up at the bookshelf above her head and she saw a booklet entitled *The Shiftology Process.*™ She immediately reached up, grabbed the booklet, and began to read. The teacher had come!

THE SHIFTOLOGY PROCESS™ by Terry-Teach-A-Lot

Changing behaviors and perspective can be challenging, and in order to improve our lives, we need to take a good hard look at our choices. The Shiftology Process™ is about shifting from what isn't working in our lives to behaviors that do work and can bring success and joy. The following mini-lessons create clarity on what steps to take to develop successful, positive results.

Shiftology™ Lesson 1: The Myth of Work/Life Balance

Isn't work/life balance what all the experts say to strive for? Do you know of anyone who has achieved work/life balance? Think about it. Probably not! Why? **Because it does not exist!** Skeptical? I'll prove it to you.

Envision an image of the Scales of Justice with the scales perfectly in balance and completely still. What's happening? Nothing! And that's what happens when life is "in balance." There's no movement, no change, no action. Stay there too long and the "Land-of-Stuck" knocks at your door. So, if work/life balance doesn't exist, what does exist? Work/life harmony.

Shiftology™ Lesson 2: Work/Life Harmony and the Five Pillars of Life

Throughout our day, we give our attention—with varying degrees of intensity and focus—to five interactive life pillars that are the foundation of how we live:

1. Health
2. Finances and Money

3. Relationships

4. Career

5. Spirituality

Dancing among all five pillars with grace and ease is the key to creating healthy work/life harmony. However, when one area is taking all of your attention, it's time to regroup and shift. Begin your big shift by answering the following challenge questions.

Shiftology™ Challenge Questions

Answer each question for each Pillar of Life.

1. What does each Pillar look and feel like right now?

2. Which Pillar receives too little attention? Too much attention?

3. What do I need to let go of in each Pillar to create more harmony among them?

4. What would each Pillar look like if I lived life on my terms instead of on what others expect of me?

5. How do I want each Pillar to look and feel?

Ana-Do-It-All took out a journal and immediately started answering the questions. She found it was challenging; however, her excitement grew as clarity filled her mind, heart, and soul. Once she finished writing her answers, she continued reading.

Shiftology™ Lesson 3: Practical Law of Attraction—The Science of Attracting More of What You Want and Less of What You Don't Want to Create Positive Results

How do you navigate your world? Is it with a glass-half-full or a glass-half-empty attitude? Your attitude, based on how you think and feel, attracts to you both good and bad. Understanding and working with the Law of Attraction offers leverage to attract those people, places, and things that you want. The following three Law of Attraction steps will help you shift and live a more stress-free and fulfilling life.

Step 1. Identify your desires. This step has two levels of intensity. Level one desires are things like wanting a great parking space or a delicious cup of coffee. Level two desires are *burning* desires. These desires create a fire in your belly, and you won't stop working until you realize them. That delicious cup of coffee can easily become a burning desire if that's what you need to move and wake up in the morning. Other examples are getting into your dream school or intense training to win a race.

What is your intense burning desire for each Pillar?

Step 2. Give your desire attention. This is where you focus, do your research, look at the who, what, where, when, how, and why, and ask yourself, "How will it benefit me?" Write down the people, places, and things that will help you attract what you want. Think about your desires, feel them in your body and own them.

Step 3. Allow. The most difficult of all three steps, true allowing happens when we let go of control and give ourselves permission to receive. The magic and miracles happen here. This is where shifting out of stress and into ease with positive expectation, trust, and belief allows desires to be fulfilled.

By answering the five challenge questions for each pillar, Ana-Do-It-All discovered a new understanding of her life. Her answers truly surprised her. She decided to begin practicing the Practical Law of Attraction immediately. She wrote the following in her journal:

Step 1: My burning desire is to learn to control stress to live with calm and ease.

Step 2: I'm giving my desire attention by reading *The Shiftology Process*™ and committing to practicing what I learn. I will take better care of myself by exercising more, eating better, taking time for myself, and learning to say "no" when appropriate.

Step 3: Allow. I am already doing a lot of what is in step two. So, what is the missing link?

She was anxious to learn more and continued to read.

Shiftology™ Lesson 4: Allow With Heart-Centered Breathing and Focus

Say the word "stress," and negative thoughts and feelings come to mind. Stress is actually neutral. Our perceptions of situations and events are what create positive or negative stress. For example, a wedding includes both negative and positive stress. So does a christening, bar mitzvah, graduation, or a new business contract. So how do you shift perceptions that create negative stress into a positive state of allowing? This quick heart-centered breathing exercise will help you control feelings of anxiety, anger, frustration, and fear that are attached to negative perceptions and get in the way of realizing your burning desires. With constant practice, positive differences soon begin to manifest in how you feel and respond to stressful situations.

Heart-Centered Breathing and Focusing Technique
(Based on the HeartMath® Quick Coherence Technique)

Step 1: Shift your attention to the chest/heart area.

Step 2: Breathe deeply in and out of the chest/heart area several times.

Step 3: Imagine something that makes you feel good. Make it as vivid as possible with sounds, colors, and images. Examples are holding someone you love or walking on a beach or in the woods.

Step 4: Hold this image and positive feeling for 60 seconds and continue to breathe in and out of your chest/heart area.

Step 5: Notice any emotional shift. Repeat until your perceptions shift and you reach a state of calm and ease.

Ana-Do-It-All immediately started practicing the five steps and, to her surprise, she began feeling calmer and focused. She felt so good that she practiced for 5 minutes and experienced relaxation that she had not felt in years. Her thirst for more information was increasing.

Shiftology™ Lesson 5: Allow With Heart-Centered Tapping

Some situations require extra help. That is when heart-centered tapping comes to the rescue. Based on the Emotional Freedom Technique (EFT) principles developed by Gary Craig, heart-centered tapping is a powerful stress-busting tool that works by "tapping" with our fingers on the same energy meridians in the body that are used in acupuncture. In addition, focus is placed on negative situations and past events that are the catalyst for creating energy blocks that prevent allowing and achieving success. Tapping works on all kinds of challenges, including pain, fear of heights, fear of success, or fear of failure. Below is a tapping script that focuses specifically on the topic of stress and re-igniting your life.

Tapping Points:

KC = karate chop (fleshy area of hand between small finger and wrist) Use one hand to tap on the other.

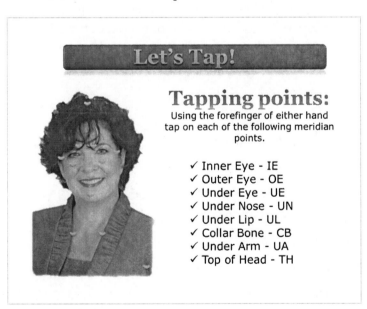

Let's Tap!

Tapping points:
Using the forefinger of either hand tap on each of the following meridian points.

- ✓ Inner Eye - IE
- ✓ Outer Eye - OE
- ✓ Under Eye - UE
- ✓ Under Nose - UN
- ✓ Under Lip - UL
- ✓ Collar Bone - CB
- ✓ Under Arm - UA
- ✓ Top of Head - TH

For the following points, use the forefinger and middle finger to tap.

IE = inner eyebrow (end of eyebrow on bridge of nose)

OE = outside of eye (outside eyebrow temple area)

UE = under eye (directly under eye)

UN = under nose (area between nose and upper lip)

UL = under lip (crease in chin below lip)

CB = collar bone (area just below collar bone on either side of body)

UA = under arm (sore spot under armpit)

TH = head (top of head)

Heart-Centered Tapping Script to Reduce Stress

Karate Chop point:

Shift into heart-centered breathing. Use one hand to continuously tap on the other while repeating the following phrase three times: "Even though I'm highly stressed and feel (choose one or all of the following words) angry, tense, anxious, worried, frustrated, and in pain, I love and accept myself."

Body-Tapping Points: Three rounds

Continue with heart-centered breathing. As you tap on each point, say the associated phrase. Add whatever words you need so it feels right for you.

Round 1 – Repeat this round as many times as necessary.

IE (Inner Eye) = I'm really stressed and it doesn't feel good.

OE (Outside Eye) = I'm allowing stress to control my life.

UE (Under Eye) = Negative stress hurts me on every level.

UN (Under Nose) = Negative stress is in my way of success. It's hurting me and everyone in my life.

UL (Under Lip) = I'm feeling angry, frustrated, worried, and anxious all of the time.

CB (Collar Bone) = My body aches with all of this stress.

UA (Under Arm) = I just can't think because of all the stress and tension.

TH (Top of Head) = I want this stress to go away.

Round 2 — Continue with heart-centered breathing.

IE = This stress is in my way of success and affecting my health.

OE = It's time for this stress to go away. I just don't need it or want it anymore.

UE = This stress is creating chaos I don't need.

UN = I'm choosing to heal my body and feel better.

UL = I'm learning how to say "no" when something doesn't feel right.

CB = I'm learning to listen to my body and respect the messages it's sending me.

UA = It's time for me to control this stress and shift my perspective.

TH = I'm choosing to see the good in things instead of the bad.

Round 3 – Continue with heart-centered breathing.

IE = I choose to think positive.

OE = I choose to feel positive.

UE = I deserve to feel good about everything I do.

UN = My body easily releases tension, pain, frustration anger, anxiety and worry.

UL = Stress will no longer control me. I control it!

CB = I'm choosing to re-ignite my life because I deserve it!

UA = I'm a Hot Mama and I choose to release stress and pain and live life large!

TH = I choose to live life on my terms.

Ana-Do-It-All thought that this heart-centered tapping was a bit weird. Her determination to become a master at living with calm and ease told her to just do it. And she did. Ana-Do-It-All was amazed at how light she felt. Her pain decreased, and she felt better than she had in ages.

Closing the *The Shiftology Process*™ booklet she whispered "thank you" to Terry-Teach-A-Lot and the wonderful information she had just learned. She felt renewed, focused and ready to achieve the success she truly deserved.

Anita Sechesky

A Registered Nurse, Certified Inspirational Life Coach, writer, speaker, NLP Practitioner and LOA Trainer, Anita is completing her Masters in Marketing at the School of Online Business, as well as Advanced Life Coaching Certificate with Coaching Cognition. She is the CEO and Owner of Anita Sechesky - Living Without Limitations. As a coach, Anita has helped many people from all walks of life break through limiting beliefs from past failures, relationships, health, goal setting, self-esteem, leadership, and motivation. She is compiling her own anthology project entitled "Living Without Limitation – 30 Mentors to Rock your World" to be released early December, 2013.

You can contact Anita at the following:

Website:	www.anitasechesky.com
FB:	www.facebook.com / AnitaSechesky
FB Fan Page:	www.facebook.com / asechesky
Twitter:	@nursie4u
Skype:	anita.sechesky
Email:	asechesky@hotmail.ca
Linkedin:	ca.linkedin.com / pub / anita-sechesky / 3b / 111 / 8b9
Pinterest:	pinterest.com / anitasechesky

TIP 8

Limitations are NOT Sexy!

By Anita Sechesky

When a little girl is born, she is a princess full of expectations and excitement. Yet so many women are not living the life of their dreams. This is a result of limitations being formed in their lives from early childhood and carrying a myriad of gender-specific traits regardless of geographical or cultural backgrounds. Often times, women respond as society would expect them to, with no recourse for motivating bruised egos, broken hearts, damaged emotions, and lost ambitions. If you desire to become the woman you long to be, then you have to let the princess go to the ball! You have to allow yourself to become all that you were created to be as a passionate female. Embrace your femininity and all your shortcomings. Then learn how to empower yourself by not being confined to the limits that can block your dreams and ambitions. As a life coach, I help my female clients take a closer look at how false perceptions can emotionally cripple and negatively affect the sexy and successful women they were born to be!

Let's take a closer look and learn how to identify the limitations and negative energy attached to them. By doing so, you can save many relationships from ending prematurely. This new awareness will help a woman embrace her opportunities to market, promote, and become successful. Once these barriers are identified as characteristics and behaviors of how we interact with various individuals, the benefits are limitless. Energy is movement; in order to see growth, you need more positive thought energy to continue moving forward or this downward heavy feeling of negativity will drain you. If it doesn't empower you or help you to be a confident person, then why are you keeping it around? We attract many of these limitations into our lives at one point or another because we feel less than perfect, below average, not attractive, or not rich or smart enough. These kinds of thoughts become blocked energy, which attracts obstacles to your success. When you identify areas in your life where hidden traps have become part of your value system, then you can address it for what it is and send it back where it needs to go. Remove the blockages in your life and open doors to greater opportunities!

For anyone dealing with a lack of motivation or low self-esteem, perceptions and attitudes are globally changing. Female entrepreneurs have stepped forward and overcome many of these boundaries successfully, including many of the co-authors in this very book! If you are still struggling with memories of bad experiences growing up, embarrassing moments, or hopelessness, you need to make a decision about what kind of life you really want to live. Keep your positive energy flowing by addressing the things that are blocking your personal value, limiting your progress, and not allowing the creativity of your sexy genius to become fully alive within you. Break off these labels and limitations. Search within your heart to discover and identify the things that have caused stagnation and even sadness. You can live a life without limitations, one that's productive and satisfying, but you need to first address these issues. If you are ready for this life, then it's time to start changing your perceptions now.

Here are some of the most common limitations I have seen women struggle with. Let's add some positive life lessons to *sexy* things up!

1. **I'm not good enough** – Negative limiting belief

   Positive Life Lesson: **I am good enough!** Why believe someone else's opinion of your value? YOU are one of a kind. YOU are genuine and the real deal. YOU are an original masterpiece. You are confident and classy! You can do anything you set your mind to. You are a winner! It's time to increase your value and believe in yourself. Let go and forgive all those, including yourself, for believing in less than you are. You ARE good enough!

2. **I'm not smart enough –** Negative limiting belief

   Positive Life Lesson: **I am a sexy genius!** Your creative intellect has been inspired from deep within your very soul. Speak to your universe and realize that you have all the power and authority to overcome all limits of your intelligence. Keep learning, be open-minded, and continually educate yourself in things that ignite your passion. Follow your heart and bring out your authentic self. Grade point averages and test scores do not determine your future outlook unless you allow them to, you sexy genius.

3. **I'm not pretty enough –** Negative limiting belief

   Positive Life Lesson: **I am beautiful and sexy!** Do you really, honestly believe the opinions of others; especially those who have no authority to give them unless you are allowing them? Maybe it's time to change your crew. The more you associate with people who look down on you or make you feel unworthy instead of your sexy self, the more you begin to believe them. Choose to believe that you are beautiful, pretty, and yes, even sexy! Be adventurous and experiment with new looks and styles that compliment your body type. Trust the opinions of others and professionals. Do research using fashion magazines. Learn about colors and skin tones, fabrics, and make-up. Embrace your femininity! Don't be shy and feel inadequate, and don't ever let another person make you feel less than the beautiful and sexy woman that you already are!

4. **I can't do that –** Negative limiting belief

   Positive Life Lesson: **I can do it!** You are intelligent, beautiful, creative, sensitive, and loving. Why can't you do what you want and be all that you want to be? If your intentions are pure and honest with integrity, there should be no limits to you finding a way. Make your life satisfying by living out your dreams. Don't let life pass you by with regrets. Visualize yourself accomplishing your goals and ambitions. Once you see it in your visions, it will become so much easier to achieve. You can do it!

5. **I don't fit in** – Negative limiting belief

   Positive Life Lesson: **I was born to stand out!** Sometimes it's better to not fit in. Leaders are meant to stand out. Leaders don't look for confidence from others, they create their own self-confidence from within by being their authentic selves. Make your mark by embracing who you are and establishing yourself as a woman of value. Love yourself more because you are your best friend. Let go of all hurtful and unpleasant memories. Free yourself from this painful trap! Only you can set yourself free! You're better than that. You've got what it takes, and you weren't made to fit in—you were born to stand out!

6. **I'm not what they're looking for** – Negative limiting belief

   Positive Life Lesson: **I am just what they're looking for!** Just because you have encountered some closed doors in your life doesn't mean the right open doors aren't there. Start believing in a better outcome. Let go of past failures. Let go of all fears of rejection. Be open-minded. Be excited. Be happy for the amazing opportunities coming your way. Envision it. Dream it. Taste it and talk about it. Attract the open doors into your life. You get to create your success first. You're just what they are looking for!

7. **I'll never find true love** – Negative limiting belief

   Positive Life Lesson: **True love will find me!** Love is universal. Love makes the world go around. Love begins with you. How you feel is what you will attract. Are you looking for your knight in shining armor? Then love yourself more. Let go of fears and all past memories of failed relationships or stories you have heard. Stop these damaging emotional thoughts from draining you. Find yourself once again. Believe in love and love will find you when you least expect it. Appreciate who you are. Do more things that you enjoy. Be creative. Dream more and think of the life you want—go ahead and write your own fairytale life now! True love will find you!

8. **Married Life is Boring** – Negative limiting belief

   Positive Life Lesson: **Marriage is passionate, secure, and sexy!** Now that you have found your true love, don't lose your sexiness!!! Your life partner is your main support system, and you need to include them in all the wonderful facets of who you are. Dedication and attention to this relationship will directly affect your confidence and self-esteem. Many men and women get so comfortable with each other after marriage that they forget who they were when dating. Bring the sexy back! You know what I mean. You had it, and you know what to do about it. Marriage can be passionate, secure, and sexy!

Can you see how easy it is to change your perceptions? If you are still struggling with any of these areas, I would love to work with you and identify what's blocking your dreams and goals. We can do this together. That's what a life coach is for. I will help you identify your passion and focus more on it. You can easily eliminate limitations and make your dreams come true. As your intention becomes stronger, positive energy increases and frequencies are tuned in, thereby attracting the right timing for business opportunities, relationships, and clients. You can now be that magnet for the right people to come alongside you, to love and support your vision and build your dreams with you. These are the people that you want to be there!

You were born a princess but when you face your limitations, you become the queen of your own destiny!

Living beyond your limitations is SEXY!

Bobbi Anderson

Bobbi Anderson started her journey in healing modalities in 2006. She is a licensed massage therapist, certified clinical hypnotist, coach, and NLP practitioner. Bobbi supports folks in chronic physical and/or emotional pain who find themselves locked in the grip of daily pain, enabling them to break out of that pattern by being conscious of what they are thinking so that they can flip the switch on their life back to the ON position! She works with clients all over the country.

Website: www.PainManagementCoach.com
Facebook: www.Facebook.com/PainManagementCoach
Twitter: https://twitter.com/BobbiAnderson13
Pinterest: http://pinterest.com/hypnosisbobbi/

TIP 9

Kick Off Your Heels: Monitor Mama's Body!

by Bobbi Anderson

As a woman, what is typically the last thing you think about taking care of? Dinner? No. Lunch? No. Physicals for the children? No. Getting the house cleaned? No. Making sure all the bills are paid? No. Typically the last thing a woman thinks about is herself—yep, there is just no time in the day to take care of the person staring back at you in the mirror every morning.

How does that sit with you? Are you ok with that?

I have news for you. There is nothing heroic about not taking care of yourself. Let me repeat that: **There is nothing heroic about not taking care of yourself!**

A woman is always putting something else first (before being herself): being a mom, a wife, a partner, a daughter, a grandmother, a sister, a friend. Very rarely do you find a woman who looks in the mirror each morning and says "I love you just the way you are and I will do my best to take care of you today." The thoughts are usually more like "What do you have to get done today? I hope you don't make any mistakes. I hope you can accomplish what you think you can. What makes you think you are smart enough to get all of that done? Wow, you look so old! Are you putting on weight?" Any of that sound familiar?

I have always loved Bruce Schneider's saying: "If you treated your friends like you treat yourself, you wouldn't have any friends." Sound right? The single most important thing that can enhance everyone's life is you taking care of yourself. That is perfectly true! When a woman's health starts to fail or her confident love for life starts to fade, so does everything around her. We are reflective of what we feel inside. We attract the energy we are living in. So if you are feeling dumpy, old, or out of energy, you will attract things into your life that reflect being dumpy, old, or out of energy.

Have you ever noticed when one thing goes wrong early in the day and you really get upset and focused on it, the rest of the day takes a similar path? Everything for that day seems to be a little "off." What I want to introduce is a way of thinking that will allow you to listen to what your body is telling you. We neglect the signals we get from our bodies. Each day, take a moment to have a conversation, an internal dialogue, with what is happening inside.

We all have hiccups in life, such as breaking a bone or having an accident of some sort. These "acute" happenings need to be addressed and followed up on. I am speaking about the feelings we get—the knot in the stomach, lump in the throat, or ache in the back. These are the signals that our bodies send us that typically are just plain ignored. I teach my clients to listen to these exact messages to become acutely aware of them. Chronic physical and/or emotional pain is triggered by us ignoring the messages our bodies send us.

Have you ever noticed that, when you encounter a given situation, person, or event, you get that same feeling? It could be a lump in your throat (you want to say something but you don't), knot in your stomach (what is happening is not in alignment with your core values), or ache in your back (feel like you are responsible for something you have no control over). So much of this can be avoided by accepting what you truly have control over and what you truly do not.

Simple, right? Well, certainly not easy. As women, we are the "fixers." We keep the day running smoothly for everyone (even if it makes us miserable).

You actually need to work on changing that. You certainly do have the control to do so. You can change anything that is directly happening to you internally.

Do you know the Serenity Prayer?

> *God grant me the Serenity to accept the things I cannot change*
> *Courage to change the things I can*
> *And the wisdom to know the difference.*

I am actually very passionate about getting people to really hone in on the message their body is giving them. Louise Hay is by far one of my favorite authors, and what a beautiful woman she is. In her book *Heal Your Body,* she very clearly defines what different ailments mean on an emotional level.

One of the biggest challenges for a woman is to stay quiet long enough to listen to what her body is telling her. If you begin to feel a slight "tingle" in your throat, why do you ignore it until it is full-blown strep throat? Much of it involves pushing the feeling away: "It will go away."

My theory is that we need to acknowledge the body when it feels something: "Ok, I feel that something is a little off. I will be more aware: What is it that you need?" So much is taking time each day to be silent with yourself and get the message that is being relayed to you via your "higher coach," that "inner wise voice." You know the one? If you don't, it is high time you get someone to introduce you to the person inside you that really has all of your answers. If you are constantly looking for answers to your problems out in the exterior world, it is time for you to kick off your heels and monitor your mama's body!

So how do you do that? Well, I have a daily routine that you can do to begin a new relationship with yourself. You will need to allow 5 to 10 minutes each morning to do this. It can be done while lying in bed, sitting on the side of the bed, on the edge of the tub, or even sitting on the toilet! It does not really matter where you are, as long as you take the time to do it.

Exercise:

Begin by just having a dialogue about what you are about to do. For example:

I will now begin my daily check-in. I am in touch with the way I am feeling and am willing to evaluate and really feel what is going on within me today.

My mind is _____
(running a million miles an hour, calm, confused, overwhelmed).

My heart is _____
(happy, sad, content, beating calmly, racing).

My spirit is _____
(light, carefree, heavy, burdened, free, caged).

These are only a few choices to fill in the blank. Whatever the first word that comes to your mind, that is where you are. **Do not overthink any of this.** This is also a very good lesson in hearing what the body is telling you. If you ask it, it will tell you. You next need to learn to listen and don't interpret it. If you hear "my mind is burdened," don't argue with it; go with it and ask what you can do to unburden your mind that day. The whole idea is to encourage not only engaging in a dialogue, but listening to it, then—most importantly—doing something about it.

If you initially have difficulty having this conversation with yourself, start by doing a short little meditation with the intention of getting in touch with the inner wise voice you have. We all have that inner voice that is quieter than all of the chatter our mind fills us with each day. By being quiet in some sort of meditation, the chatter quietens a bit; by asking for wise council, you will begin to add volume to the deep thoughts you have, which will give you the clarity you are seeking. There are dozens of meditations out there. I have some on my website.

Take time to take care of yourself. Remember to look yourself in the eye each morning when you look in the mirror. No one likes to be ignored, and that is just what you are doing when you avoid eye contact with yourself in the mirror. Mirror work is one of the things my clients have the most difficulty with. It is surprising how many folks cannot look themselves in the eye in a mirror and say they love themselves. Sad, is it not? We are all God's creatures and we all have God's life in us. How can you look God (or the power you believe in) in the eye and not say "I love you"? You are that power, my dear friend. You are made of that same energy.

You can find my free meditation recording "Feather Relaxation" at: http://painmanagementcoach.com/free-stress-relief-audio-relaxation/

Lady Jazz

Lady Jazz is a visionary with the mind of a mogul and a heart for serving others. This multifaceted "mompreneur" is a mastermind, adding to the lives and success of those that cross her path. She is an Executive Director for National Professional Women of Color Network; host of her upcoming Online Radio & TV Show, founder of Ladies Night Out, an empowerment support group; and she is also launching her non-profit organization in 2014.

Contact her at Lady.Jazz.Dozier@gmail.com or Jazz@pwocn.org for additional information.

Connect with her on the following social media websites:

LinkedIn: www.linkedin.com/in/jazzdozier/
Facebook: https://www.facebook.com/jazz.dozier
Facebook: https://www.facebook.com/LadyJazzEnt
Facebook: https://www.facebook.com/pages/Girl-E-Time-TV/ 247463495319025
Facebook: https://www.facebook.com/PWOCNSS
Twitter: https://twitter.com/LadyJazzD
Pinterest: www.pinterest.com/ladyjazzd
Website: www.LadyJazzEnt.com
Website (Skincare & Wellness):
http://mindbodyandsoul.soulpurpose.net
National Professional Women of Color Network – www.pwocn.org

TIP 10

Forty and Fabulous: Keeping it Sexy, Savvy, and Successful

by Lady Jazz

Embrace your 40
- Fear is only as deep as the mind allows
– Japanese Proverb

So many women cringe at the thought of turning forty? Like many of you, I felt the same way. However, the aging process didn't bother me as much. I was fearful of the **"what if's"**. Having unexplained health issues for over five years didn't make it any better. I suffered from heart palpitations, high blood pressure, and weight-gain, stress then depression. I was flat-out mortified, no lie. I was guilty of allowing that nasty little four letter "F-word" to tap into my fabulousness and steal my joy. By the way, the "F-word" is FEAR! Gotcha!

For many, it's the changes in appearance that we fear. You know... the gray hairs, cellulite, the couch potato syndrome, the lack of interest from the opposite sex or significant other, fine lines and wrinkles etc. Then there's the medical side of things: breast and cervical cancers, menopause, hair thinning or loss, increased cholesterol, weight gain or loss, fatigue, vaginal dryness and decrease in skin elasticity. I could go on for days about some of the things we are faced with and yes, it can be pretty scary. If you're in your twenties and thirties, you may pick your jaw up now. Don't worry my friend; many of these fears are avoidable. YOU hold the key and have the ability to kick that **F**alse **E**vidences **A**ppearing **R**eal to the curb.

Here are 5 easy tips you can use yourself or share with someone who could benefit from them. The sooner you get started, the better.

1. *Be pro-active with your health; get started now! Don't wait until you turn thirty or forty, go see a doctor regularly and have some peace of mind.*

2. *Take care of your skin! Moisturize and exfoliate your skin daily. Our skin is the largest organ on our bodies and is on the frontline for us. Take care of your skin and it will take care of you. I use an all-natural product line, Soul Purpose products, which have no parabens or synthetic sulfates. Excellent for all types of skin.*

3. *Take time out for yourself. Do whatever it is you love doing!*

4. *Change eating habits and eat healthier. I get great recipes from Pinterest.*

5. *Exercise, Exercise, Exercise! You will notice the changes in your overall health and appearance when you exercise.*

You are Fabulous!

- But the most exciting, challenging and significant relationship of all is the one you have with yourself. And if you can find someone to love the "you" you love, well that's just fabulous!
–Sex in the City

Repeat after me...MY forty is FABULOUS! If someone would've told me to say those words, ten or twenty years ago, I probably would've laughed myself into a coma. Ladies, we are the new thirty and a force to be reckoned with I might add. More SAVVY, SUCCESSFUL, and SEXIER than ever. We got S.W.A.G.!

Let me share a secret with you: **WE ARE ALL FABULOUS!** You see many of us get caught up in the notion that we have to be born with a silver spoon in our mouths; we have to look a certain way, be a certain size to be fabulous. That's BS! The truth is, being fabulous is really how you view yourself and how you treat others. Do not worry what other people think or allow them to define you. It's all about liking, loving, and being true to you.

How to Keep Your Sexy
– A great fit your physique is nice, but it's self-confidence
that makes someone really sexy
–Vivica Fox

Repeat after me…Sexy is a state of mind. It's about what makes you comfortable. You don't have to be naked or a size 2! Don't get caught up in society's "quick sell" remedies. It's all about how you carry yourself and your confidence level. I will say, keeping in shape is the best thing that you can do for yourself, no matter what your size is. Truth is, we all have sex appeal and it comes in all sizes! Do YOU?!

Here are 7 steps that I encourage you to try. Feel free to send me your feedback and let me know what worked for you.

1. ***Buy something new, step outside the box.*** *Try something more tailored that compliments your shape, size, and age.*

2. ***Experiment with your make-up.*** *Try some lashes, they are in style and can make a huge difference in your appearance.*

3. ***Change your hairstyle.*** *Try something new! Experiment with wigs.*

4. ***Maintain good hygiene.*** *People appreciate a good smelling woman.*

5. ***Pamper yourself.*** *Love you first!*

6. ***Be on point!*** *Dress to impress (YOU).*

7. ***Impress your mate;*** *wear something sexy to bed and try something new, it can make for a great start to your day (wink).*

Keep it Savvy
– When you know better, you do better
- Oprah Winfrey

Knowledge is power, ladies! Don't settle! Stay on your game. In today's society, being socially, relationally, and tech savvy plays a huge part in your success. This is one of those times that you want to "keep up with the Jones'." Ha-ha!

Here are 5 tips for you to utilize that will assist you in becoming savvy.

1. *Find out about the latest technology. What are others using?*

2. *Join a social network.*

3. *Seek out advice from your peers, a coach and other professionals.*

4. *Expand your horizons. Step outside of your circle. Create new connections; build relationships both online and in person.*

5. *Get a mentor or life coach. Learn from them, don't reinvent the wheel. Work smarter not harder!*

Achieving & Maintaining Success
- If you want to soar like an eagle, then hang with the eagles!
Remember chickens don't fly!
– Dr. Quindola Crowley

Most people want to be successful, but the truth is only a few will achieve that goal. Success doesn't come easy. There are also downsides to attaining success, too. So prepare yourself! Always have a PLAN B and DON'T STOP until you get there!

What does success mean to you? I recently asked a good friend to define success. She replied, *"Being able to live my life with purpose and on purpose. Living out my dreams and accomplishing the goals I've set for myself personally and professionally."* I couldn't agree more! Success comes in many forms and we all measure success differently. When coaching, I tell my clients not to get caught up on what "others" say, rather go with your own feelings. You should always celebrate your successes no matter how big or small. I believe when doing so, it motivates you to push even farther. Once you have reached one goal doesn't mean you stop there, keep going onto the next!

Here are 10 steps to get you started.

1. ***Develop a plan,*** *have a goal in mind or a dream. Talk to a mentor, gather ideas and formulate strategies and do some research; study other successful people.*

2. ***Get Clarity!*** *You should know what success means to you and what that looks like for you. I suggest writing it down on paper to get a clear picture.*

3. *Plan your steps! Make sure you have the necessary tools to carry out to your goal based on what your plan is and the steps needed to get there: i.e. for my non-profit I have several steps needed: filling out paperwork, putting together a board, find funding, search for location etc... Don't reinvent the wheel, find out what has worked for others that you admire and go for it!*

4. *Set a timeline! When do you want to achieve your goal? If you're a mother, you may need to be flexible. Things happen, but don't stop! Plan for setbacks, they will occur!*

5. *Execute! No procrastinating! Get started immediately, even if it's little by little... YOU CAN DO IT!*

6. *Avoid Distractions! They are bound to happen, but you must stay focused. Keep them to a minimum and know that you may have to make some sacrifices to get there.*

7. *Obtain accountability partners to help you stay on task. This is a HUGE piece and is what has led to my SUCCESS!!!*

8. *Create a support system! Surround yourself with positive and successful people that will pour into you and believe in YOUR vision. THIS IS A MUST! Naysayers will KILL the DREAM!*

9. *Delegate Duties! It's ok to ask for help. Work with people that you know are trustworthy and will go to bat for you!*

10. *Network! Network! Network! This can cut your time and money in half when done properly and help spread the word faster. You might even pick up a few experts that are willing to validate you along the way. Bartering does wonders. You heard the saying... I'll scratch your back if you scratch mine... Well start scratching!*

~ Be Blessed, Stay Fabulous! Lady Jazz ~

Heather Love Eden

Heather Eden is a Certified Health, Fitness and Lifestyle Coach, with a BA in Creative Writing. Heather is a Fitness and Well-being Writer for Demand Media Studios, and has a coaching business called Complete Wellness Coaching. She coaches online to women of all ages on health - in balance with diet, exercise and lifestyle. Heather can be reached through her website and other links:

Website: www.heathereden.com
Facebook: www.facebook/completewellnesscoaching
Twitter: www.twitter.com/heatherloveeden
Pinterest: www.pinterest.com/heatherluveden

TIP 11

How to Sizzle through Motherhood without the Burnout

by Heather Love Eden

Motherhood can be very challenging, especially if you are juggling a career on top of it. Without proper time management and self-care, moms can easily fall behind on energy and momentum. We need lots of good energy to succeed daily. We also want to feel centered, sexy and in control of ourselves without fueling the body with anxiety and fear.

Since anxiety is an outward expression of fear, the challenge is to reverse the fear by acknowledging the worry and realigning yourself with uncompromising values. Discover your truth. "Whenever you experience this kind of anxiety, it's a call for your own growth. Congratulations! You have entered a customized opportunity designed specifically for your personal growth." (Hal Edward Runkel, LMFT, *Screamfree Parenting*). The objective here is to identify your values and practice them daily.

Moms want to feel sexy for their significant other, and 'wow' them throughout life. But, how can a mom feel sexy and desirable when feeling run down? They can't! The key is to fill the body with clean energy (clean diet, positive thoughts and right actions) and exert clean or positive energy, and keep refilling the cup with love and self-care. If mom is in a rut, she must confront her darkest fears, and ask herself difficult questions. Being honest takes courage, and you got it! Values should stay in the frontline and act as a shield for the heart and mind. (Remember to think before reacting). Everyday must begin in thankfulness and end with satisfactions (;-). Did I make my heart smile today? Did I make my children's hearts smile today? Did I make my significant other's heart smile today? Did I make the world smile today? Please don't feel overwhelmed. This is not my intention. (Excuse the Southern Dialect!). No mama can accomplish their to-do list daily. And don't worry! If you're reading this book, you are an amazing hot mama! So, here are some sassy, sizzling tips to help you find the fire inside to feel and look smoking hot!

Take one step at a time.

Get moving to be patient. Sometimes everything can seem out of grasp. As moms, we are climbing mountains to accomplish *the list*- daily chores, personal needs, child's needs, dinner, relationship connections, career objectives, etc. Overwhelmed yet? Taking one step at a time is the way from start to finish, and you can't cram everything into one day. Set daily intentions in the morning, make lists and check them off as you complete tasks. You are an amazing mommy!

Schedule primary food activities.

This is everything you need to thrive outside of keeping a clean diet. Healthy relationships are a must to feel your best. Drama brings frustration and negative emotions. Understanding yourself first will help you understand others. Make positivity your top objective when associating with others. People appreciate positive people rather than those who complain day in and day out. Be aware of resistance and learn from it. Nurturing positive relationships in your life will bring you joy and laughter.

Regular exercise is a must do. Finding time to get moving is another piece of primary foods. Exercise enables your body to properly function, move out toxins and enhance mood. Aerobic means to increase oxygen. Everything good is associated with that word when it comes to caring for your body. We can all use more oxygen. Adding aerobic exercise 3 to 4 times a week will help you feel your best! Also, add some strengthening exercises 3 to 4 times a week to tighten that bod!

A fulfilling career is another hot commodity. When I say career, I mean working at something that brings you joy. It goes along with taking one step at a time. A fulfilling career doesn't happen overnight. Some of us work for a long time to figure out what actually makes us tick. Others find it very naturally. Just don't get impatient with yourself while you're on the search. And don't give up! Try different things, and don't be shy to try. Finding your passion and living it, keeps the fire burning inside. That's hot!

Having a spiritual practice is vital to our spirit/life. Our breath is related to spirit. "The wind blows where it wants to, and you hear its sound, but don't know where it comes from and where it is going. So is everyone who is born of the Spirit." (Jesus). Keeping an open mind, being comfortable with uncertainty, staying thankful, forgiving and in practice of connecting with the Uni-verse or God is a very beautiful place to be. Being connected with the Divine is like being attached to the vine as a grape. You feel whole, a part of the whole, uniquely divine, delicious, tempting, perfect, completely at ease and open for growth. Love is attainable, and it is very attractive.

Eat healthy foods.

"Let food be thy medicine and medicine be thy food." (Hippocrates). No one's perfect. But, you must resist the temptation to eat junk food, processed foods and fast foods. You have to read labels and become a food investigator. That's smart! Intelligence is sexy. Eat all natural and choose organic foods when possible. Eat a variety of fruits and vegetables daily- raw if you want or cooked lightly. Choose whole grains, lean proteins, nuts, phytonutrients and clean oils. Cut down on dairy, cut out nicotine, reduce caffeine and moderate alcohol as much as possible. Drink water! Cut out sugar as much as possible, especially sugary drinks and sodas. Make room for super foods! Juice daily and get the healthy glow! Beautiful skin is sexy!

Ask for help.

I know you feel like superwoman, but everyone needs help. Define your problem, research what other moms have done, read about it and hunt like a tigress for a solution. However, connecting with others in order to find solutions defines community, and the experience builds knowledge, confidence, trust and relationships. You're not alone. Speak up when you need something. Having your homework done on the subject always gives you an advantage. Moms need help too. But, going into a situation blind can bring unwanted stress and complications. Hire an expert! You can gain momentum and self-respect by investing in yourself. Self-respect is very attractive.

Get rest.

You cannot heal and recover properly without adequate rest. You need 7-8 hours a night. Rest is also taking a break when you need it. Recall the times when you are moving non-stop for hours at a time, and your body is nudging you to stop and rest. Listen to it. Trust your body. It's better to listen to your body for cues to rest and to re-energize, rather than to suffer the consequences of your body's defenses. Prevent the burnout and keep those creative juices flowing!

Breathe frequently.

Breathe through stress. Breathe through pain. Breathe deep in the mornings and set your intention for the day. Allow your body to take in more oxygen. Your body will thank you. Focusing on the breath helps you keep your cool. Breathing through stressful situations helps you make mature decisions, which will lead to healthy relationships. Breathing through tough times also helps endure trouble. The breath is the passageway to your center. You can find it practicing yoga. You can find it through meditation and stillness. Mindful breathing is another way to find your breath. Being mindful of your breath while you are moving along from task to task will help reduce stress, and enable you to observe thoughts and feelings as they come and go. A self-aware person takes control of their mind, discarding negative thoughts and feelings. "Healing is as natural as breathing, and therefore the key to healing is a lifestyle that optimizes what the body is already doing." (*Superbrain*, Deepak Chopra and Ruldoph E. Tanzi). However you find your breath, find it. It's our gateway to self-realization, self-control and a calm center.

Don't compare yourself with other moms.

I can't count the times I've seen moms in public who look so well put together, calm, balanced and friendly, while their kids were nagging or whining about something. I used to wonder how they did it. Later I realized (when I became a mom) that moms have to be a little fake sometimes, until they learn how to actually *cope*- C-Curious, O-Observant, P-Principled, E-Energized. Comparing yourself with other moms creates negative feelings. Remember your values, be a grape on the vine, breathe and understand it is your own beautiful, unique journey. Be authentically tolerant of your own journey and where you are in the moment. Then, do the same for other moms. Every mom has the same struggles. It's all about the timing. Friendships happen when the same struggles align and both moms are open to growth. Be open to other moms for friendship and support.

Spend time with supportive people.

Make friends with people who celebrate with you and compliment your good qualities. If you feel like you have to prove yourself worthy for someone's time, then they aren't worth your time. Knowing your self-worth and practicing self-care will attract like-minded people. Seek to understand the law of attraction. It will help you learn why certain people come into your life.

Write in a journal.

Writing in a journal is extremely beneficial for moving through thoughts and feelings that need to be released. We seek counseling because we need to sort and dispose of thoughts, memories and feelings that are trapped in our cells. Counseling is recommended, especially through difficult times of change and emotional disruption. However, journaling daily, weekly or even a few times a month can really build up momentum for the healing process, while seeking to maintain a whole body-mind balance.

All mothers, single or married, want the best for their children. They want to feel they are doing a great job, all the while feeling desirable and valuable. Listening to your body, observing the mind and creating healthy routines that fit your lifestyle will lead you to complete rejuvenation and wellness for the whole body and mind. Health matters and it should be the first priority for moms who desire to sizzle and shine!

Frenetta Tate

Frenetta Tate is a Certified Empowerment Coach, Motivational Speaker and President of EmpowerMe365™, a boutique company designed to deliver lifelong innovative, content-rich, value-infused tips, tools, key insight and strategies to entrepreneurs to promote dynamic and undeniable success in life and business. The focus is to encourage and promote business alignment and whole life sustainability for entrepreneurs. *EmpowerMe365™'s* vision is to shape entrepreneurs into powerhouses of Influence and Inspiration through speaking engagements, teleconferences, workshops and live events.

Website:	www.frenettatate.com
Facebook:	https://www.facebook.com/Empowerme365
Twitter:	http://www.twitter.com/frenettatate
LinkedIn:	http://www.linkedin/in/frenettatate
Pinterest:	http://www.pinterest.com/frenettatate
Instagram:	http://web.stagram.com/n/Frenetta/
YouTube:	http://www.youtube.com/user/frenettatate
Google+:	https://plus.google.com/102744129603810749207
Skype:	frenettatate
Email:	frenetta@frenettatate.com
Phone:	281-728-7547

TIP 12

Spicy Tips to Conquer Self-Sabotage

by Frenetta Tate

Self-sabotage is when we say we want something and then we go about making sure it doesn't happen.
–Alyce P. Cornyn-Selby

I lived a vicious cycle of self-sabotage for many years. It permeated every area of my life. I was my own worst enemy. I learned that I had to deal with the root of my issues: internal struggles that needed to be addressed before I could be at some level of success in this area. I had to answer the whys and come to understand one fundamental principle:

Unless you deal with the root problem, solutions are temporary; issues will return and freedom will not remain.

Merriam Webster defines sabotage as "an act or process tending to hamper or hurt." I define self-sabotage as a mixture of opinions, approaches, feelings, actions, and sentiments that form a block to success by working against your own self-interests.

Basically, you work against yourself, not for yourself. In many cases, self-sabotage acts as a self-fulfilling prophecy where you create an expectation—whether negative or positive—about circumstances, events, and even people that affects your behavior toward the circumstances, events, and people in such a manner that causes those expectations to manifest in your life.

What Does Self-Sabotage Look Like?

I was the example of a self-saboteur. I allowed many fears to paralyze me. I had a fear of success, of failure, of being a failure at success (that is, once I was a success, I would not handle it well), of what people would say about me, and that I was not good enough or smart enough. I did not believe in my abilities or potential. When something went wrong, I was always blaming myself. I thought I was the problem. I wouldn't move forward in many areas of my life because of fear. I would back down, buckle under, and not stand up for myself. I missed a lot of opportunities for growth, development, friendships, and valuable connections because I had a very low opinion of myself and that opinion was the driver for all of my actions, words, and interactions with others.

It was that low opinion I had of myself that blocked me from being an influence and inspiration in my life and business. I allowed it to block every success, every great opportunity, and every great relationship that tried to positively infiltrate my life. It also affected my expectation attitude. We tend to foster and promote behavior that aligns with our expectations.

A Spicy Example: A sales person who does not expect to get a profit-sharing bonus will not follow up with her clients on a for-sure order, do everything she can not to make a sale, or attend training courses to increase her knowledge for a product her clients want to buy all because she does not expect to get a profit-sharing bonus. Because she is dead-set on sabotaging herself, she does not realize that a profit-sharing bonus is available to her if she just does her job. Thus, when profit-sharing bonus time comes around and she doesn't get one, she says, "See, I told you that I wasn't getting a bonus." Well, she made that happen by not doing her job, and she didn't do her job because she did not expect to be rewarded. Her behavior said that she did not "deserve" it so she acted in accordance with her low opinion of herself. Her low opinion drove her to do everything she could to sabotage herself.

Self-sabotage deals with three things: self-esteem, self-worth, and self-confidence. These are the drivers of your life.

1. Self-esteem is your overall emotional evaluation of your worth.

2. Self-worth is having a sense of value and respect for yourself.

3. Self-confidence is having an assuredness in your own judgment, ability, and power.

Self-sabotage will either (1) block your success or (2) manifest before you reach success.

I've been presented with many opportunities in the past and sabotaged them because of my mindset at the time. I realize that now because hindsight has perfect vision, right? For a long time, I did not believe in myself. Yes, other people believed in me, other people thought I was the "bomb diggity," but I didn't. I eventually learned three things:

1. It does not matter what other people believe about you. *If you don't believe it, it will not help you.*

2. It doesn't matter if people think you can do great things. *If you don't believe it, you will do NOTHING.*

3. It doesn't matter if other people see greatness in you. *If you don't believe it, you will not reach your full potential.*

I came to understand that, in order for me to be all that I am destined to be in my life and as an entrepreneur, I had to conquer self-sabotage and so will you.

Conquer Tip: Recognize when you are sabotaging yourself by staying in tune with your interactions and responses to what happens to you. Base your response on the pure truth of the situation, not what you might be incorrectly assuming. When you can recognize it, you have an opportunity to turn it around.

A Spicy Story: A well-known entrepreneur was coming to Houston to do an event and asked me to be one of the featured speakers. I said "yes!". Several weeks went by, but I did not follow-up. Then I saw a flyer about the event and I was not on the flyer. I immediately contacted the person and did not get an answer. So, I resigned myself to the conclusion that I would not speak at the event since I did not reach the person (after one call—I did not even give her a chance to respond). I shared the situation with a friend, who encouraged me to "stay open."

Now, my attitude toward the situation was that I wasn't going to call again or even worry about it. I had resolved that "it just wasn't my time," but I was wrong. I was sabotaging my opportunity. How do I know? All it took was a phone call and I was in, but I was "resolving" instead of standing up, following up and taking advantage of an opportunity that I already had!

Thankfully, I recognized what I was doing and stepped up. I spoke at the event and touched lives! If I would have allowed myself to just "resolve," I would not have fulfilled my purpose of touching lives through the talk I gave at that event. I would have sabotaged an opportunity once again. I won't do that again.

Conquer Tip: Practice self-observation on a daily basis, evaluate yourself objectively, and adjust accordingly. When you are objectively evaluating yourself, you see areas of improvement that reflect on the good things you did for yourself.

A Spicy Story: I sabotaged a past relationship because I resorted to what I now call "labeling your present or future by your past experience" and not allowing my present to stand on its own in addition to not allowing the new person to stand outside of the shadows of my past. My assumption was that it would all be the same as the last relationship, so I wasn't looking to do anything new; I wasn't thinking differently or changing my behavior so I could have a different result. I was stuck in that mindset and, as a result, the person walked out of my life. He didn't stand a chance against my issues. Of course, I learned from that and I don't do that anymore. Now I have a healthy relationship.

How we show up in relationships with others is just one of the ways we sabotage ourselves. We also sabotage ourselves through our words, behaviors, and actions. We are often not even conscious of it. Our conscious minds tend to carry out the right actions and work toward our goals, but the subconscious part of us pulls out that mixture of opinions, approaches, feelings, actions, and sentiments that are misaligned. This misalignment paralyzes us.

Conquer Tip: Take steps to overcome self-limiting behavior. Stop limiting yourself with your actions and words. Release relationships that are limiting and hindering your growth and development. When this misalignment happens, all of our fears and feelings rise to the surface and we start working against ourselves again. Why?

Unless you deal with the root problem, solutions are temporary; issues will return and freedom will not come.

You might be sabotaging yourself verbally, financially, physically, emotionally, and relationally. There are many ways in which we do it. Some of us are in every area of life and some are just in a few, but no matter where you are, you can improve, you can do better, and you can truly live a victorious life. It is all up to you and your choices.

Conquer Tip: You must be real in order to deal. To conquer anything, you must be honest about where you are and what you truly need. Being honest with yourself will help you improve in the areas of need.

Ask yourself these questions and answer them truthfully:

1. Do you beat yourself up verbally or mentally over a mistake? Call yourself names, like idiot, no good, or stupid?

2. Do you keep repeating the same patterns?

3. Do you trample over the good that happens and focus on the bad?

4. Do you tend to look more at your faults rather than your strengths?

5. Do you usually blame yourself when a problem occurs in your life?

6. Do you constantly compare yourself to others? (e.g., I should be further along, Patty is doing way more than me).

7. Do you find yourself ready and willing to help others, to give them all kinds of advice but not to take the time needed to solve your own problems?

8. Do you do something to botch things up to get out of an opportunity or event? (e.g., run late on purpose, make up an excuse, pretend to be sick, not show up to an event and lie about why).

9. What do you need to conquer self-sabotage? How can you be victorious instead of a victim?

If you answered "yes" to any of these questions, you might be sabotaging yourself. We don't have to live this way. We can conquer this behavior by adopting actionable principles and renewing our ways of thinking. It is our thinking that's driving our sabotaging behavior.

Conquer Tip: If we can get our minds right, we can get our lives right. It all starts with your beliefs and what you think about yourself. Align your beliefs with a positive outlook on life.

Ten Spicy Tips to Conquer Self-Sabotage

1. Believe that you are worthy of success. Embrace it for your life.

2. Believe that you have great value. Only you can devalue yourself.

3. Believe that you are more than enough. You have exactly what is needed.

4. Believe that you are one of a kind. Comparison does not apply to you.

5. Believe that you are not always to blame. Stop assuming everything is your fault.

6. Be a problem solver. Benefit from your own advice and wisdom.

7. Believe that you are talented. Don't despise what you've been given.

8. Stop devaluing and belittling yourself in front of other people. Accept a compliment by saying "thank you"—no further commitment in deed or speech is required.

9. Choose not to focus so much on your faults; highlight your strengths and work on your faults, but do not place your faults above your strengths.

10. Accept yourself as you are. You might make a mistake, but accept the responsibility for it and move on. Don't beat yourself up about it. Let it go. Don't get down on yourself and sabotage yourself further with your words.

Believe in yourself and your ability to conquer self-sabotage. Adopt these tips and put them into action in your life daily. As you do this, you will be well on your way to being a powerhouse of influence and inspiration in your life and in business.

AnYes Van Rhijn

AnYes is an international leadership expert. Her program "Make Things Happen!" helps women succeed in their business or career. Her "Intentional Leadership" program helps international managers and executives (both men and women) be successful and fulfilled while serving as a role model for those around them. Her clients describe her as a leadership booster. They say that working with her is transformative and has a profound positive impact on their personal and professional lives.

Email:	agnes.van-rhijn@cclsconsulting.com
	agnes@conscious-leaders-academy.com
	agnes@successfulwomenacademy.com
Skype:	tclacademy
Websites:	www.successfulwomenacademy.com
	www.conscious-leaders-academy.com
Social media:	www.facebook.com/agnes.vanrhijn
	www.facebook.com/SuccessfulWomenAcademy
	www.facebook.com/consciousleadersacademy
	www.fr.linkedin.com/in/agnesvanrhijn
	www.about.me/tcla
Twitter:	tclacademy

Be a Leader: Make Things Happen in Your Career or Your Business!

by AnYes Van Rhijn

When I look back at my life, I'm amazed to see how long I stayed in the dark! There are no such things as regrets here; some people stay in the dark much longer and some even never get out of it, but the important thing is that I did get out of it. When I say staying in the dark, I mean not taking charge of my life and letting others and circumstances decide for me. I think that my awakening process started on my 40th birthday. When raising my glass of champagne for a toast, I said: "To a year of change!"

I had no clue what I really meant, but deep down inside I knew that something had to happen. Although some things did change, it took me another 6 years to start understanding what this meant. Due to a series of circumstances, I did not finish my studies. I am what we call a self-made woman: Because I was a good performer, I managed to climb the ladder in the corporate world and went from my first job as a secretary at age 18 to administrative director of Europe for a worldwide firm 25 years later. I was very good at what I was doing, but despite making a very good living and being proud of what I had achieved, what I was doing was not fulfilling me. It was just a job! When I started realizing that, I also became conscious that all I had been doing was grabbing opportunities as they appeared (I admit that it could have been worse). I had never decided what I wanted my career to look like, and it was becoming clearer and clearer that my career at the time was not what I would have chosen. But what would I do instead?

I still had no idea until I attended the first module of a coaching training (paid for by my employer). It was an epiphany, one of those "ah-ha" moments! From that moment on, I knew that this was what I wanted to do, but even more I wanted to have my own business. That is when my real journey of transformation started. I say transformation because that is really what it has been; there has been a before and an after. People who knew me then are astonished at how different I have become. That journey is the foundation of the work I do today. I have set up my own coaching and mentoring business. To do so, I have developed myself as a leader.

Today I am on a mission to help as many people as possible do the same because I do believe that we can all be the leaders of our lives, if not the leader of others! Given that I also strongly believe in the power of the ripple effect, I know that if each and every one of us create our own success and fulfillment, together we can make this world a better place.

What I have discovered in my own journey and through more than 5 years of working with my clients is that, in order to be successful and fulfilled, we need to set an intention, raise our level of awareness, shift our mindset to be a winning one, make conscious choices, commit to our goal, and collaborate! That is why I have developed a framework that I now use with all my clients in both my "Make Things Happen" program and my "Intentional Leadership" program. The 5C framework (Clarify, Clear, Create, Commit, Collaborate) is a holistic and transformational approach that looks at all areas of life, even if the work I do with my clients is primarily focused on their career or their business.

Although there is of course not enough space in just a chapter to explain in full detail what I mean with these elements, I am going to introduce you to the first two steps of my framework as these are fundamental and will help you start moving in the right direction so that you can start making things happen for you!

Clarify (Raising Awareness)

Most coaching or training programs, when talking about clarifying, refer to clarifying your project. I believe that, before clarifying your project, you need to raise your awareness: Who are you really at this moment in life and what is important to you? As said by Brendon Burchard, the author of (amongst other books) *The Millionaire Messenger*, at the end of your life the only important thing will be your answers to the questions "Did I love, did I live, did I matter?" You can only answer those questions in a positive way if you are conscious of how you are living your life. In order to do so, you need to raise your general level of awareness! The thing with women in particular is that, because we tend to put others' interests and well-being first (our kids, our significant other, our boss), there is hardly any room left for us, not even mentioning the fact that a lot of us think it is selfish to take time for ourselves, assuming we are even thinking we are worth it!

So let's go back to who you are and what is important to you. It might be the first time that you do so in your life, but for once, take the time to step back and reflect. I like to start by putting you in the bigger context of the world. What would your ideal world look like? If absolutely nothing would stand in the way, how would you like to contribute to that ideal world? From there, let's look at you: What are you passionate about? What are you secretly dreaming of? What are your values? How do you live them? What are your needs (that is usually a tough one!)? And what boundaries have you set into place to ensure those needs are respected? What does your basecamp look like: Who are the people who support you? When you are able to answer these questions, you can start connecting to the essence of who you truly are.

Clear (Shifting your mindset)

In that first step of clarifying who you are and what is important to you, you likely encountered what we in coaching refer to as your gremlins or limiting beliefs (you know—that little voice that keeps reminding you that it is impossible or that you are not worth it or that keeps asking you who do you think you are?). As long as you just accept them (as you always did) without challenging them, nothing will change in your life. So let's instead look at how you could start clearing (and thus shifting your mindset) everything that stands in the way. Although there is much more to cover, there are 4 essential areas that need clearing for most of us:

Your thoughts and your language

Everything and its opposite exist in the universe (ying and yang, black and white, heavy and light, etc.). In fact, they are two opposite extensions of the same thing. What you focus on expands, and your thoughts and your words create your reality. What do you focus on? Do you behave like a victim or an actor? Do you always look for what is not working or do you gladly see what is working? Do you express (assuming you do) what you don't want or do you express what you want instead? What would your life look like if you could shift your thoughts and your words, thereby shifting your reality?

Your physical environment

Our physical environment also determines how we feel in our body and in our mind. How much of your physical environment corresponds to what you would want it to be? Do you live in a home/city/country you enjoy? Do you feel good there? Is your home all clutter or does it have a peaceful touch to it? How much of the stuff have you inherited from former lives or from family or friends? (I write this looking at a gift from a friend that I still have in my living room after so many years, although I've never liked it; I promise, the moment I finish this chapter, I will remove it!) What would your life look like if the moment you enter your home you immediately felt at peace and resourced?

Your toxic relationships

Whether still in this life or whether transitioned to another one, some people have a toxic impact on us. Whether it is/was their intention or not is not even relevant (although if it is, it will require forgiveness); what is relevant is the fact that it has negative consequences for us. Let me give you an example of something that happened to me. When I was a teenager, my father once told me that I should not behave as if I were Brigitte Bardot (for those of you who don't know who she is, she used to be a famous French movie star in the 60s). I grew up and never thought of it again until a few years ago when I was working with a coach to understand why my business was not being as successful as I wanted it to be. She said to me that I needed to be more visible. Bingo! There I was, in a workshop with 300 women, just enrolled in a program called "Stars Plus" realizing that my father had told me not to stand in the spotlight, not to be a star! He never meant to block me, but my entire life I had done my best to be ... invisible. (I have of course, since worked on that, and this is no longer an issue for me). So, who are the people in your life who have that kind of impact on you? Is there anything you can do to "get rid" of them? If not, what can you do to let go so that it doesn't affect you anymore? Do you know that we are the average of the five people we see most? What would your life look like if you were surrounded only by people who support you, who stretch you and who have a positive impact on you?

Your relationship to money and success

Our relationship to money is a reflection of our relationship to others and everything. I'm not going to enter into more details here because you will find a great chapter on that topic by one of my co-authors in this book. It is an essential part of my framework and, more specifically, of the clearing step. What would your life look like if you were at ease with making lots of money and being successful?

Answering those questions isn't easy, and certainly not on your own; the best is if you can get the help of a mentor and if you can leverage the power of a support group of like-minded people. Also make sure to understand that this is a process. You are not going to wake up and have all the answers overnight. I even believe that it is a lifetime process. We must keep peeling the onion. My experience and that of my clients has shown me that, without working on those two steps (clarify and clear— namely, raising your awareness and shifting your mindset), whatever you want to create (give a new turn to your career, set up your own business, or whatever else it is that you want to do) is doomed to fail. Raising your awareness and shifting your mindset are mandatory steps if you want to start revealing to yourself and to the world the leader you have in you. If you don't work on these steps first, it is as if you were trying to build a new house above an existing one without first identifying what to keep, what to revamp, and what to add.

There are also two essential things that you will need to ensure that you are heading in the right direction and that you stay focused: intention and progress.

Intention

Without a clear intention, all the above will get you nowhere. At every step and every question, you need to be clear about the "what for" to explain why you are doing it. For example, before you start the clarify phase, set the intention that you want to gain clarity as to who you are and what your needs are. In the clear phase, before you start it, set the intention that you want to understand what stands in the way of your success and from there decide that you want to clear what can be cleared and accept what you cannot change. These are only examples. In everything you do, be clear about your intention and consciously set it.

Progress

Human beings don't like change, but if you want different results for yourself, you have no other choice than to start doing things differently. Doing things differently can feel very awkward, but that is simply because it is not yet a habit. It has been said that behavior has to be repeated for 28 days in a row (although I have also read 21 days) before it becomes a new habit. But doing something that isn't familiar yet is easy to drop when we don't yet see the results we seek. That is why it is once more very important that you are very conscious of the progress you make; when you don't see progress, ask yourself what you need to change or adapt for it to work. I always tell my clients to behave as if they were in Edison's shoes. Edison had to create an amazing quantity of light bulbs that did not work before he created the one that did. These light bulbs that were not working were never failures for him; instead, he saw them as something to learn from so that he could improve the next one, and he just never gave up!

TIP

What will get you started is to identify something that you want to change. Here is an exercise that I give to my clients to help them do so:

1. Answer the question: "What is a situation that I have experienced today that is no longer serving me?" (It might have worked in the past or perhaps never worked, but you are becoming conscious that this is no longer okay). Start journaling about it.

2. Once you have identified that pattern, recognize how uncomfortable it is; if you don't, you will find tons of reasons to keep it in your life. Also connect to the cost of not addressing it. I don't mean necessarily financially—although there might be a financial cost to it—but the cost in terms of energy and negative emotions. There is always a cost linked to not addressing an issue.

3. With that cost in mind, decide what you want to do to change that situation.

4. With that decision in mind, choose the first little step that you can undertake that will bring you closer to the results you want to see.

5. Once you have decided what that step is, set a daily intention that focuses on it (example: Today I will do ABC to come closer to achieving my decision of XYZ).

6. At the end of the day, ask yourself, "What was my intention? Did I do it?" If the answer is yes, congratulate yourself. It's important that you become aware of your successes and that you identify the benefits that you have experienced because that is what will motivate you to replicate a new behavior that is not yet anchored. If it did not work, ask yourself why it didn't work. How could you twist it so that it could work for you?

Repeat this every single day, and you will start seeing things shift for you.

To your success and fulfillment!

Kayoko Omori

Kayoko Omori is a spiritual coach, truth provocateur, and life purpose accelerator. Using her *"intuivation"* (intuition and innovation), she guides *on fire* biz owners, messengers, and brilliant eccentrics in making a difference in the world without sacrificing their integrity. With uncommon speed and care, she helps melt "boulders" standing in the way of her clients and their glorious purpose. Long-term stuck issues are her specialty. She is also a succulent wordsmith, visual artist, and poet with two children.

Website: www.kayokoomori.com
Email: ko@kayokoomori.com
YouTube: K-Star TV

TIP 14

"End Struggle, Be Your Own Guru" A Sure-fire Formula for Getting Unstuck

by Kayoko Omori

Decide to Leave the Struggle World

Naming the devil is *golden*. Why? Say Sam had chronic constipation from birth, but he didn't know it by name. If constipation is his norm and all he's experienced, what's the chance of Sam seeking a "cure"?

So here it is. We have chronic "bliss constipation" on our hands. From when we were young, many of us saw our parents, teachers and society inhabit the world of constant struggle and problems. Bliss constipation was customary. We dutifully and diligently copied their constipated-ness to ensure our sense of survival and belonging. So we are a bit cemented and glued to the ground in the struggle world. In other words... we're STUCK.

Notice Your Stuckness In It

Most of the time, you are usually positive and laid back. You know what you're doing in many areas of life. Except in this particular aspect.

"I'm usually really _____, but when it comes to _____, I just stop feeling like my normal self. It's weird."

"I feel like a total failure in _____ (but I dare not show it)."

"I get so jealous and out of control when I see _____ _____."

You feel helpless, a bit shut down. Or you might have that foggy, confused kind of stuck. Everything seems to be going well. Your life is like a wonderfully predictable movie.

"I know I'm really fortunate compared to most people, but I don't think people know how _____ I really feel inside."

"Isn't there more to life than this?"

Determine Where You're Stuck: Introducing *The Bliss Thermometer*™

How 'In the Flow" Are You?

The Bliss Thermometer™ helps you rate how much "flow" you experience in general as well as in specific areas of life. It intuitively gives you a reading of how "warm" you are, from 1 (cold as ice = severely dissatisfied and dangerously stuck) to 10 (steaming hot = amazingly blissful and fulfilled). Just as you have your normal range for body heat, you have your own "home" temperature range – your normal tolerance level for bliss and happiness – which, despite occasional fluctuations, stays about the same over a period of time. When you feel lower than your home temperature, usually it is accompanied by a period of "high", so you average out about the same.

Example: You go see your abrasive mother-in-law for the holidays and are moderately triggered, so your bliss temperature plummets from your normal 7 down to 4. But when the visit ends, you're so happy about being back, plus your husband suggests a mystery date, so that the rating stays at 9 for a few days.

Temperature Taking Procedure

I will first guide you in taking the temperature for your life in general and then for specific life areas. No underarm necessary, just your imagination! I will sprinkle a little magic dust over this book and through and in between the words...*pinnng!*

I declare that you are totally, easily accessible to your super GPS within, a.k.a. your *gut-feeling!* Pretend that you are doing this assessment for your very best friend. You're 200% curious, but not personally invested. Make believe too that you can't *think* your answer, but you are simply picking up some radio transmission through your invisible antennae.

For printable Bliss Thermometer worksheets, go to
http://kayokoomori.com/free-gift/

Step 1

On a scale from 1 to 10, what does your Bliss Thermometer™ show your current temperature for your life in general?

Let a number come to you effortlessly. Jot it down.

Step 2

Moving to Life Areas:

- Money
- Career/Job
- Your Business
- Health and Well-being
- Body Image
- Purpose and Passion
- Romantic Partnership
- Family Life/Parenting
- Creative Self-Expression

Using the same principle, what is your current temperature for your Money area? Jot down the number that "pops up." Continue this, going down the list with each life area. (*Note*: If you don't have a romantic partner, then you can rate how dissatisfied you are that you don't have one or that you lost one recently. The same goes for business, parenting, and creativity. Be flexible.)

Step 3

Compare the temperature rating for "life in general" against those for "life areas". Note the life areas for which the number is particularly lower than the number for life in general. Circle up to three areas.

Step 4

One by one, allow the stuck feeling that a circled area conjures in you. Let the stuck feeling and emotion (anger, dissatisfaction, shame, helplessness, tightness, etc.) arise *gently* and *just intensely enough* so that you know the specific issue(s) within this life area. Write down up to 2 issues per life area.

Case Study

To demonstrate how this actually works, I will use a client's example, who we will call Kate Starr.

Kate's Results: General temperature 7

Relationship (temp: 3)

1. lack of intimacy
2. money behavior

Business (5)

1. overwhelm
2. avoid networking

Body Image (4)

1. feel heavy
2. clothing problem

For printable Bliss Thermometer worksheets,
go to http://kayokoomori.com/free-gift/

Get to the Bottom Line

Review the issues you jotted down for the stuck life areas. Pretend that they are all related somehow. Do not "think." Tune in to a deeper awareness where a bigger "a-ha" picture is already present.

Case Study

Kate realized that she is not trusting of her live-in boyfriend somehow. She works harder and earns more than he does. She gained weight after they moved in together and created a joint bank account. She knows she can be successful, but she is being sabotaged by her crippling sense of her changing looks. After all, if she earns more, would her boyfriend stop earning as much and start "taking it easy"?

The Cause of Stuckness: Your Inner Mother Wolf's Way of Protecting the Wounded Cub

The fact is, we are getting something valuable out of whatever stuckness that looks, feels, and sounds awful. We create drama to camouflage, delay, or deny something we don't want to face.

Case Study

Kate discovered that her not feeling beautiful in her body, while it is painful for her, served a few important purposes. It kept her from feeling sexy enough to have intimacy with someone she couldn't yet fully trust. It also kept her from magnetizing more business and, hence, income. More money might expose that her boyfriend is with her more for convenience than for love. Kate didn't want to be confronted with finding out the "truth". Why? Because she wanted a relationship badly. She didn't want to be alone. Her stuckness served to ensure that she would not be alone.

Let's turn now to *your* purpose. And I need your radical lovingness within to step up here. Ask your intuition what the ultimate freak-out place is that you get to avoid by remaining stuck in this way. No forcing. Wait for an emerging awareness, and receive. Write it down.

For printable Bliss Thermometer worksheets,
go to http://kayokoomori.com/free-gift/

Thank You and Farewell

This stuckness wasn't random, nor was it your or anyone's fault. It is important now to acknowledge the profound service that it offered for deep within it is the energy of pure concern and protectiveness, like that of a dutiful mother. So we complete this specific point of struggle with gratitude.

Case Study

Kate, with her hands on her heart, would take a deep breath fully present, and say: "Thank you, all my stuckness, for trying to protect me from feeling alone and empty inside."

What would you say? Place your hands on your heart: "Thank you, all my stuckness for _____."

Moving Into the Flow World

Cross the Boundaries

If only Kate would try not to feel alone, would you say that everything would be ok? Well, in fact, it might push her right back into the struggle world. You're at the borderline between two worlds. You have to decisively release "trying" or "trying not to." This is the time to relieve the stuckness from its job. Fire it with utmost integrity: "Thank you. I am ready to release you from that duty. You don't have to protect me anymore. I am curious, and open to feeling this sense of emptiness, if it comes."

Get Your Home Address

Now, as you put your powerful step into the flow world, you need to know where you're going. Otherwise, the familiar old world starts beckoning you back (remember, most people don't live here). So you need to know where you're stepping into, exactly – a new home address that belongs to you and only you.

But how?

Anchor firmly into the depths of your heart. Ask yourself what you really want. You will know your true heart-destination if what you want is something that—if you were to have it—you wouldn't ever need any more struggles or drama. Drop in, deep breath. What would that be for you?

Case Study

Kate: "Of course I want to be in a relationship, but what I really want is to feel loved and appreciated for who I am."

With hands over your heart, declare and claim this new abode.

Be Your Own Guru: Support from Your Future Self

Go back to step 4, where you find the issues for the most stuck life areas. In this final stage, check in with your future self (now a seasoned resident in the Flow World) for solutions and action steps regarding the given issues. Feel into your heart destination statement. Imagine tapping into your future self, who is *already there!* Allow her to support you.

Case Study

Kate's statement was: "I feel loved and appreciated for who I am."

Her Future Self

relationship

lack of intimacy: "When you feel desire naturally, you make love; if not, you don't."

money behavior : "close joint, have separate accounts"

business

overwhelm: "find out where you're most overwhelmed, delegate"

avoid networking: "start feeling good, a few new dresses would go a long way, red is a good color"

Hone In On Your Greater Purpose: The Power of Your Inner GPS

So now you have pretended and imagined a lot, retrieved hidden information, and dialogued with your future self. That was real work. You experienced genuine shift. Except it cost nothing, it was fast, and it was completely safe. You barely even moved.

Do you know what you did?

You used your own built-in guiding system, your inner GPS that's grossly undertapped in most people. But those who heed their calling and become a conduit for greatness are not, for the most part, most people. If you are reading this, chances are, you aren't most people. Your inner GPS is just as good as anyone else's. The difference comes in when you start to *exclusively* rely on it.

Have the courage to bloom—the way you are so designed—into your fuller, more joyous fragrance. No. Matter. What. Freely. Boldly. Moment to moment.

Hot Mama IN (HIGH) HEELS

Marja Norris

CEO of Transformation, I AM, Marja Norris is an author, wealth advisor, financial planner and executive mentor. She is currently authoring a book for release in 2014, _Dress for Success from the Inside and Out_, which she pens with candor and levity as she teaches how to _rock_ it to success in particularly male dominated businesses. Marja serves on the board of HAVEN, for victims of domestic violence. She lives in Michigan with her husband Jerry, is the mother of two amazing adult children, Larry & Kristen, and two adorable dogs, Bailey and Bella.

Website:	www.marjastyle.com
	www.marja@marjastyle.com
Email:	runmarja@aol.com
Facebook:	www.Facebook.com / MarjaStyle
Pinterest:	www.Pinterest.com / MarjaStyle
Twitter:	www.Twitter.com / MarjaStyle
LinkedIn:	www.Linkedin.com / MarjaStyle

TIP 15

Secrets Revealed: Be the Best Dressed Woman in the Room!

by Marja Norris

It's confession time!

Haven't we all been caught out in public, not looking our best, only to turn around to see someone we know? Or what about that unexpected visit from an important client or acquaintance, wishing we could quickly become invisible? Have you ever been stuck in that rut of not having the time or energy to look your best, only to have it come back to haunt you later on through photos? We get busy, and so often as women, we put ourselves on the back burner.

How would you like to change your ordinary into *extraordinary*?

It's easy and I'll show you how! I've loved fashion since I was three. Although I am in finance, which I also love, I have long studied women's fashion and it has allowed me to scrutinize countless professional women and to observe what works – and what doesn't work. I attended the Summer Intensive Fashion Design Program at Parsons in New York City, taught by professors that have also trained some of the world's most famous designers.

Let's be clear here: **I believe that all women are beautiful!** We can all do a little tweaking to **bring out our best.** My goal here is to lift you up by revealing some of my quick and easy secrets to looking good, having a more professional appearance, and therefore, loving life even more. **Let's get started...**

Add a "Fashion Folder" to your Closet!

While sifting through magazines or searching the internet, if you see an outfit that catches your eye, rip out or print the photo and toss it into your fashion folder! Accumulate perhaps 10 to 20 photos, covering various looks like errand Saturday, work clothes, and going-out attire. I recommend a subscription to Style Magazine or the like, as outfits are presented in detail, from top to bottom, including accessories. Great additions to your fashion folder.

When you're short on time and have that "I can't find anything to wear" moment, you can reference your folder for ideas on a quick *go-to outfit*. Even though not identical, it'll start the juices flowing on your creativity to find what to wear now. I guarantee it!

How to shop the Catalog and Internet

It's always best to try on clothes in a store. In today's available times to shop, it's not always realistic. If you're Internet shopping, save yourself the time and trouble of returns by utilizing this simple trick. Unless you are one of the lucky souls of nature that looks like a model or movie star, make a reality adjustment when deciding on a purchase. I'll give you an example. I'm vertically challenged (in other words, short). I cover the face of the gorgeous model with one hand while with my other hand, covering the portion of the model's legs to my approximate height. (That's a lot of covering up in my case). I now have a realistic idea of what I can expect to see in the mirror once the outfit is on me, and not a model that would look good in a potato sack.

Know what Colors Look Good on You

Here's a fun social opportunity for you and a girlfriend. If you've never had an expert help you find your ideal colors - without makeup, in daylight – now is the time to find out what colors work best for you. Go with your friend to a fabric store and purchase about 20 or so assorted color swatches. I recommend Joanne Fabrics, which carries 20" by 20" swatches that are perfect for this exercise. If you're not sure what colors to start with, check out the web before you shop. Just type "clothing for skin colors" in the search section. An excellent tool is the website *Color Me Beautiful*, by Carol Jackson.

To start, take a mirror and place it near a window. Bring a chair to the mirror so that the daylight is on your make-up free face. Now, glide the swatch in front of you to see what colors look good. Through the process of elimination, the colors you keep will fall into a guide: autumn, winter, spring or summer colors. Got it?

Now take the swatches of your ideal colors, cut them into 3" by 3" squares, punch a hole through the swatches with a hole punch, and slip the squares onto a key ring. This is your Swatch Watch. Now it's easy to toss in your purse or glove compartment and have on hand when you shop. It works!

I had my colors done by an awesome stylist in New York City. Although my closet was full of black clothes, I found out that black is not my best color. Although I didn't toss all of my black clothes, I did pick up scarves and blouses I can pair with them, thereby reflecting the autumn colors that best compliment me. With the right colors, I don't look so drained anymore. Promise yourself that you'll follow this rule when you shop. You'll never look at clothes the same way again!

Speaking of scarves, they are the least expensive way to stay current on trends, rather than replacing your wardrobe every season with the "in" prints or colors. (Make sure your scarves line up with your Swatch Watch!). Now, when the next season comes and trends change, a $30 scarf - instead of a $300 outfit - goes to Goodwill.

Looking Like a Million Bucks for a Lot Less!

Are you on a budget and don't have the funds to buy new clothes? Let me tell you how to pull this off - and smile to yourself as your friends or coworkers pay full price for the same exact garment. You don't necessarily have to shop at the high-end department stores, although browsing through their sales racks can produce some quality bargains. Instead, start at T J Maxx, Marshalls and similar stores that bring in designer brands. They carry an array of designers such as Calvin Klein, Ralph Lauren, Tahari and Diane von Furstenberg, just to name a few. Pull out these labels. Ignore the rest.

Target stores host continuous 'specials' from well-known designers such as Prabal Gurung, Kate Young, Jason Wu and Phillip Lim. See what your wardrobe is in need of and the next time you're at Target, check it out! Even Neiman Marcus has collaborated with Target, producing nice merchandise at incredible values, especially around the holidays.

Larger retail stores like The Limited, Express and Banana Republic have the ability to buy fabrics in such large quantity that they are often able to negotiate deals with their fabric manufacturers, and then pass those deals onto you. Also, these types of stores may offer a 'test market' item on a limited basis. A garment that should go for $300 may be test marketed at $69. Ask the manager if there are any special pieces in. This is particularly true of the larger cities.

Learn HOW to Spot the Trends!

In addition to style magazines, check out the stores or websites of H & M, ZARA, and Forever 21. (Tip: Some of the Forever 21 stores are geared towards younger women but it's worth looking at, as they show what the trends are for all ages by posting "New Trend" on their garment racks). These retailers are known to follow the runway shows for quick turnarounds and can have items similar to what is seen on the runways on their retail floors in a matter of a few weeks. Other high-end retailers do as well, but it seems these three are particularly quick. Also, a website called *SSENSE* is great for following trends!

Marja's Golden Rules

I hope you've picked up some great tips so far. I'd like to wrap up this chapter with my Golden Rules:

1. **Never buy anything without looking in a rear view mirror.** Carry a small mirror with you when you're shopping. If it doesn't compliment the back, it ruins the front. Put it back!

2. **If it's not hip or elegant, don't buy it.** Now that you've figured out **the look you're trying for,** you see something and say to yourself, "Isn't that *so* cute?!" or "*so* adorable?!" If your first thought is not "That is so hip or so elegant", for example, then don't buy it. Otherwise, you'll just be adding more of the same to the closet you already have and not what you are trying to expand upon.

3. **Find a good tailor.** A garment is only a good deal if it fits perfectly. Have it altered to make the outfit *yours.*

4. **Toss what doesn't fit.** Whether it has shrunk (yea, right...) or it never felt right in the first place, if you don't love it, retire it. Bring a box home from the grocery store, put the items in the box where you know you can still get to them, then date and label the box. Next season go through the box of items. I'll bet you didn't miss them - and you're now feeling able to donate them.

5. **If you don't wear it, return it.** If you buy something and find you don't wear it within *two weeks*, return it, unless you bought it for an upcoming wedding or special occasion. I have found that if I've not worn it within the two-week rule, it really isn't one of my favorite pieces. Therefore, I only end up wearing it a couple of times a year, and that's a bad investment. I'd rather invest the money in a Roth IRA or exchange the outfit for a pair of quality shoes that I'll get more use of.

6. **The condition of our shoes and handbags matter.** Speaking of shoes, be aware of their condition. Shabby shoes will ruin even the most expensive or well put together outfit. Shoes tell a lot about a person, and the same is true for handbags.

I hope you enjoy the ride on your **transformation into the new you!** It's about awareness, confidence and attitude - and I know you can pull it off! **Believe in yourself!** You'll soon see a shift in how people around you believe in you, too. That's where the fun begins!

Lorii Abela

Lorii is a multi-awarded, international leader and speaker and an expert on soul mates. Co-author of the best-selling Amazon book *Speaking Your Truth Vol. 3*, Lorii is originally from Manila, but lives in Chicago and is helping thousands of expatriates find their soul mates using her powerful techniques. Over the past seven years, she has tirelessly promoted the Law of Attraction and has authored several articles on it. By the way, she has also found her soul mate!

Website:	http://HowCanYouFindLove.com
Membership Site:	http://www.manifestingyourtruelove.com/
Facebook:	https://www.facebook.com/HowCanYouFindLovewithLoriiAbela
Twitter:	https://twitter.com/#!/howcanufindlove
LinkedIn:	https://www.linkedin.com/company/2451359
Google+:	http://gplus.to/manifestingmydestiny
YouTube:	http://www.youtube.com/user/asianspy168
Instagram:	http://instagram.com/loriiabela
Pinterest:	http://pinterest.com/howcanUfindlove/
Klout:	http://klout.com/#/howcanufindlove/

TIP 16

Hot Secrets to Being Attractive to Your Soul Mate

by Lorii Abela

Finding a soul mate is always about first changing your inner self. Most people keep looking outside of themselves, but when you cater to your inner needs, only then can you be truly attractive. I learned this lesson in my 40s—not that it's a bad thing, but there are times when I wish I'd found my soul mate a lot sooner. Yet I trust the universe and its way. Come to think of it, how else could I be sharing my story with you right now?

I was like most other people when it came to love—always looking for a solution outside myself. My mission in life was clear: to find a soul mate in New York City. It seemed simple enough. After all, with a population of 8 million people, New York was bound to have something for me. I went to nightclubs, partied with singles, and even signed up on dating sites. Believe you me: I was kept busy during those years, answering messages, chatting online, talking on the phone, and pretty much being my own personal secretary. I had so many dates that, on the weekends, I didn't even have to cook! I had a bit of success, and a couple of relationships even lasted a year each, although most fizzled out after the first date.

When I moved to Chicago, my life changed. I found out about the Law of Attraction and finally realized that the only way to change my situation was to do an "inside job." This is what I learned, and I hope my experience will help you find the person you will love for the rest of your life and who will love you back with as much or more fervor.

Know Thyself

For a long time, I thought something must be wrong with me as a person. I mean, come on! I was beautiful, smart, and educated and had everything going for me. So why couldn't I find Mr. Right and keep him for life?

The first thing I learned was that I had to bundle up all my insecurities and throw them into the deepest part of the Chicago River—not good enough, not rich enough, not pretty enough, not smart enough ... everything. Remember one thing: as far as your soul mate is concerned, wherever he or she might be right now, YOU ARE PERFECT JUST THE WAY YOU ARE. If that's worth writing in capital letters, then it's worth memorizing. Your soul mate isn't going to dismiss you just because of your "perceived" faults. He or she will love you exactly the way you are right now. The following exercise, created by Byron Katie to help people face reality and embrace it, will help you understand what I mean.

Exercise

Make a full list of your self-limiting beliefs, then put them through the questions below:

Question 1	**Is it true? (If 'no', then skip to question 3)**
Question 2	**Can you be absolutely sure that this is true?**
Question 3	**What happens when you believe that thought, and how do you react?**
Question 4	**What kind of person would you be if you didn't have that thought about yourself?**

You have to stop being your own worst critic. You really do. Create a new reality that is in sync with your new beliefs about yourself. This is the only reality that matters, so burn the old one so it never haunts you again.

Here's an exercise that might help: Put a large, loose rubber-band on your wrist; pull it and snap it against your skin every time you start criticizing yourself. In a surprisingly short amount of time, you'll learn the lesson. Your pain, when linked to your self-criticism, will help you get rid of that nasty habit.

Love Thyself

I've been part of so many international organizations whose only purpose was to serve others that the words "love thyself" seemed like an alien concept to me. Although I had taken up these responsibilities voluntarily, something inside me was urging me to take care of myself first.

I eventually discovered that the secret to doing good work for others is to first love yourself enough to recognize and fulfill your own needs. This isn't the same as being selfish, because that would mean thinking *only* about you and no one else. Self-love is the first step to understanding the concept of loving others as you love yourself. Even if you're not religious, these words make perfect sense. It encourages you to nurture your own spiritual, mental, and physical needs before you tend to the wounds of others.

When you're on an airplane, the flight attendant advises those with children to put on their own oxygen masks first. Doesn't that make sense? You can't help your child if you are gasping for breath.

Exercise

Once a month, do something exclusively for yourself. It doesn't matter what it is: Go to a day spa and pamper yourself, take a weekend trip to a place where luxury is the name of the game, treat yourself to a vacation with a close friend, even a long hot soak in the tub with some great music to keep you company might be just the thing you need to rejuvenate yourself. Be in tune with the inner you. As you relax on your special day/weekend/week of self-love, try to find some quiet time to listen to your inner voice. Put that iPod away and listen to what your heart is telling you. Meditation isn't about going away to the mountains and forgetting the world; it's about keeping your mind open to what your spirit is telling you. You can do it in the bathroom, just before you go to sleep at night, or even in the morning as your wakefulness slowly overtakes your senses.

Follow Thyself

When you hear your soul speaking to you, the natural tendency is to be skeptical. After all, society keeps telling you to think of others first, right? So why should you follow your own heart and its passions? Doesn't that lead to a life of debauchery and self-deceit? Certainly not! Your heart will never lead you to a life of disarray; it's your head that does that.

Are there things you regret not doing? Well, do them now! It's your life we're talking about, not your kids' (if you have any) or even your parents'. Read my lips: It's your life, so live it the way you want. Now, obviously, this should come with a disclaimer that you shouldn't totally disregard the people you love when you live life on your own terms. Yes, we do have obligations to fulfill and promises to keep, but never do these things at the cost of your own happiness. That's what it means to follow yourself.

Exercise

Make a list of all the things you've ever wanted to do: learn to zumba, learn a foreign language, go bungee jumping, start a website, go to Acapulco, swim with sharks (in a cage, of course), talk to your mom… it could be anything. Don't worry about the hows and whens or the ifs and buts, just make the list.

When I first moved from New York to Chicago, I knew all of two people. I knew I had a passion for organizing people with apparently unrelated backgrounds into groups, so that's what I did. It was a hit! I was happy because I had pursued my passion, and I ended up with more friends than I could handle. I also wanted to add some zing to the experience, so I called it "Women of the World–Chicagoland." It was such a big hit because it sought to promote internationalism and friendship, and it helped women from hugely different backgrounds find some common ground. In no time, I had gone from stranger to having a Rolodex full of friends. With all the activities, information exchanges, and cultural blending, these women had finally found "home." Here's what we in Chicagoland focus on:

a) Exchanging cultural ideas

b) Developing ourselves and our interests

c) Starting businesses

d) Learning about and promoting music and art

e) Serving the local community

Promote Thyself

Practice "Joy"

Have you heard the expression "give respect and you'll get respect"? It's the same with relationships: If you want to be loved, you have to be lovable, and that essentially means giving the other person "your own brand of lovin'" before you can expect theirs in return.

Don't think that you'll be doing this just for the benefit of others. You are the main beneficiary of this technique. What this involves is you being a conduit for joy—the kind of joy that sends out "like" vibrations (pun intended, of course) to others. When you're joyful and happy, this is exactly what you will attract back to you. This is where you become the one who benefits the most.

Exercise

Analyze yourself through the day and assess your emotions. If you feel down, find something that will perk you up. Do you have a favorite song? Play it. Do you have a "happy place"? Go there. Do what it takes to bring yourself back to a state of joy. It's tough, because the regrets of the past and the cares of tomorrow will try and bring you down. Don't give up; don't give in.

Match Thyself

This might sound like a strange thing to do, but it worked for me. It can work for you, too. If you can, "own" the qualities that you'd love in your soul mate, then your perception of relationships will change forever.

Exercise

First, make a list of all the things you would love to have in a soul mate. Now, try to mimic those qualities for a day. Try to do it more often so it becomes your second nature. You'll see what I mean the longer you practice. The primary objective of this exercise is to look at life from another perspective—one that you respect and love. In the process, you'll understand what kind of person your soul mate is likely to be.

In a sense, you are trying to manifest your match by attracting what you love about a potential soul mate. If you want to attract generosity, be generous; if kindness is what you seek in a soul mate, be kind to someone. Once you learn to do this, you'll automatically attract people of the same wavelength. And never forget: The person whom you attract next could be your soul mate and partner for life. Don't you think it's worth it?

In my case, I can vouch for each of these exercises because, eventually, my soul mate practically landed in my lap! It could be the same for you.

Shelley J. Hawkins

Shelley Hawkins, MS, is founder and creator of The Self Connection™ liberating the spirit of entrepreneurs and professionals from the inner obstacles to their potential—who they are—through creative and intuitive coaching, mentoring, writing, and speaking. Her studies and training include business, communications, energy psychology, Theta Healing®, EFT®, and the neuroscience of transformation with Dr. Joe Dispenza. She earned her Masters in Holistic Nutrition and wrote her thesis *Changing the Vibration of Food*. Her published work includes *Law of Attraction Magazine* and her award-winning ezine.

Subscribe to her *Monday Wisdoms™* at www.theselfconnection.com; schedule her for a speaking engagement or apply to coach privately with her at theselfconnection.com or info@theselfconnection.com.

Facebook: www.facebook.com/theselfconnection
Twitter: @shelleyhawkins1
LinkedIn: http://www.linkedin.com/pub/shelley-hawkins-ms/35/426/906

TIP 17

Destiny's Edge: The life that wants you as much as you want it

by Shelley J. Hawkins

Like the space between the notes makes the music,

We discover our potentials in the space between our actions.

The surrender, the listening, the thinking, the trust,

Renewal, rest,

And pregnant pauses.

Destiny's edge is found here

In the daring space we take,

We make, we fear, we resist, we receive,

To calibrate with the life that wants us

As much as we want it to be our life. ©

~Shelley J. Hawkins, *Monday Wisdom*™, June 17, 2013

Out of a chunk of marble abandoned decades before by another artist, Michelangelo sculpted the statue of David and later remarked that "David was already in the marble." All he did was reveal him. Yes, Michelangelo decided where to chip, sculpt, and sand, where to start, and when to stop. He chose the scene, the rock, the vision…and apparently he listened.

Michelangelo was commissioned to sculpt a statue of David, but he took a different approach than his artist predecessors. He chose to depict David in the intensity and anticipation prior to battle, with the slingshot over his shoulder, rather than in the relief and triumph of victory, with Goliath's head at his feet.

I wonder what the statue would have become if he'd chosen to depict another scene? If he had worked with a different chunk of marble or merely acted on the marble, willing it into form instead of seeing himself as engaged with it? Would it be as profound? As life-affirming? Would it have moved so many?

We already know that destiny is created, yours and mine, but the dynamic that Michelangelo alludes to for creating David is a listening as much as an action for his artistry to come through. This is the dynamic we play with in shaping our destinies.

Imagine Michelangelo deciding where to make each chisel, to sand a bit more here. What if I make this hand larger? Lay the sling here? What will it look like if I remove this? I wonder what Michelangelo would point to as mistakes? How each one became blended into the statue that millions now view in awe, powerfully moved?

Life moves us in the direction that chisels away at what covers our uniqueness and true nature, the parts we made up to survive, avoid vulnerability, and project an image as well as the parts we constructed to protect ourselves, be loved, approved of, rebel against, control, and avoid pain. It can mean pain and it can mean ecstasy.

"This isn't the way I would have chosen for this to happen," a former client said the other day. His intention was to leave his job and start his own business. Being laid off before he was ready wasn't part of his plan.

We make our choices, and life shapes them. We listen and realize we are also listened to. Destiny's edge is found here. Doors open and close as we participate in our own masterpiece—our life, ourselves.

The rain fell on the windows of the coffee shop as I listened to a woman whose story is familiar in these times of great shift. She moved through the recent span of four short years with intention and action: Divorced, she left her long-time home behind to live on her own for the first time, got a new job, went to school, earned her degree, and started a business; and realized her child was suddenly an adult. You can fill in the blanks with your own transitions. On this side of the change with everything in motion, she wrapped her arms around her handbag as if for comfort, toying with the leather handles in her fingertips, and wondered aloud if this is what she really wanted. The in-between of transition is minus the ironic comfort of misery and a step or few away from the stability and new norm of a dream fulfilled.

She had been so determined in action, she wondered if she'd really listened or done what she thought she had to. She questioned the steps she had taken to stay "in action," wondering aloud if it is what she really wanted.

"Intention and surrender are not in conflict with each other," I said. "They're synergistic. It is how you unfold your potential."

In a pregnant pause she looked at me as if to absorb the idea. Her whole body relaxed. She was good at goals, action, and staying ahead of her fears, the conventions of so-called potential. But space? Listen? Surrender?

If we want to live our version of the "real thing"—life, love, creative fire, to the bone fulfillment, potential, giving, happiness—we must courageously turn into our fears instead of pushing through them, turning away from them, ignoring them and use them as a catalyst for self-knowing to make space for the life that wants us as much as we want it.

I wonder how my friend in the coffee shop will morph the steps she's taken into her continually emerging destiny. Every masterpiece has imperfections. Like David, we stand in awe of them. At any moment we can morph our choices in a new direction.

Listening means space. Artistry is uncertain. Michelangelo couldn't be certain of the outcome of each chisel. Many squirm with the idea opting for the illusion of certainty by filling it up, being decisive. But that's the slow road of evolution, of shaping your destiny. We can be decisively uncertain. We can decisively listen and wait.

"I feel exhausted and numb," said Olivia, an artist and client. Connection at any cost had been her unconscious motto. When space showed up in her life, she would close the gap with projects, working both sides of the relationship, social commitments, and contracts. There was money that must be made, aloneness to avoid, accomplishments to attain, but they didn't lead to self-knowing, into that infinite well of creative potential. She couldn't trust life to come to her, and it was exhausting her.

Destinies, after all, are unique. We create them and we are shaped by what we create. Herein lies the edge: to courageously leave the space and listen to what wants to be revealed in us, like David and Michelangelo. At times that might mean minutes, months or years.

Calibrating to the life that wants you

The power of a destiny built on making space to listen is that you awaken latent abilities and hidden possibilities, opening a way of thinking you haven't traveled before. Intentions come from what you know. Listening invites us into the unknown where all possibility awaits.

"Emptiness is the source of all creative potential," said just the right person at just the right time. *I know that*, some part of me said. *Yet I don't know that or I wouldn't be looking for a way out of it*, said me in another voice. When the marble that hides our truest and magnificent nature is being chiseled away, the inner transformation of ways of being that you no longer need, it can take all you are, all you have, to leave the space for it to happen.

When you trust space, you cultivate trust in movement. It becomes conscious. Deliberate. When you can trust yourself with space, you can trust yourself with your future—beyond your imagination. For the uninitiated it might look like a selfish act, nonsensical in a world that worships making-it-happen. But this is the dynamic of artistry, masterpieces that span centuries and personal destiny that lives on in essence and in the hearts of others. The funny thing about this kind of alignment is that, when you're listening and acting on your inner voice, it will move more mountains in the smallest action than a lifetime of massive action without it.

Calibrating to the life that wants you as much as you want it matures your relationship with destiny. You learn to trust in what you don't know, to rest and surrender, that you really are enough as you are right now, and that choices from the past can be morphed into your masterpiece. Any quest for potential delves deeper into the goodness of your true nature to bring it to the surface and give it away in an infinite array of possibilities.

Calibrating to your Destiny's Edge

Try this:

1. I often ask my clients what intuition they have been receiving that they have ignored. With one client in particular, we would clear the pattern that was keeping him in a particular state of life, and the dialogue would change and he would open to possibility. Then I'd ask him what thought, idea, direction, or feeling has been coming to mind that he'd ignored or that he thought didn't have credence. He wanted to stay "productive" rather than "listen." Inevitably he would say what it was and his next step was clear.

2. Do the same for yourself now. What is one thought, feeling, direction, idea that has been coming intuitively, fleetingly, and repeatedly to mind that you have ignored?

3. You can also look for ways you stay busy that are no longer meaningful.

4. You can also look at your fears and where you are "closing the gap" instead of listening. Are you afraid of being alone? Afraid of letting go of a dream, a way of being, a relationship? Afraid of not making a contribution? Afraid of being taken advantage of? Afraid of not making enough money? Afraid of more goodness and expansion?

5. What action do you stay in to avoid the fear or the feeling behind it?

6. Behind the door of fear is your potential. The fear is an old voice, and your true nature is pushing it up to be dissolved.

7. Listen.

Michelle Stewart

Michelle is a passionate and inspirational leader in the field of music, video making, and internet marketing. Most widely recognized for her drumming videos, Michelle is also the force behind teaching people how to reach their global audience, speak from their core (authentic self), and clone themselves through video. Her videos are watched in 170 countries with more than one million views.

Website:	www.MichelleStewart.com
Website:	www.BodhranExpert.com
YouTube:	www.YouTube.com/BodhranMasterclass
Facebook:	www.Facebook.com/MichelleStewartOfficial
Facebook:	www.Facebook.com/BodhranExpert
Twitter:	www.Twitter.com/MichelleStewart
Pinterest:	www.Pinterest.com/mstewartpage
LinkedIn:	www.linkedin.com/in/michellestewartofficial

TIP 18

The Authentic Clone: Taking the mystery out of reaching your global audience

by Michelle Stewart

Back in 2008 I was a stressed-out, overworked mother and wife—the typical exhausted musician and teacher. In two short years, I went from being a depleted soul with a voice condition that left me barely capable of speaking to launching my first video product, making more money in ten days than I had the entire previous year teaching full-time. Now my videos have more than one million views and are watched in 170 countries.

How did I do this?

I cloned myself.

By creating red-hot YouTube videos (teaching the Celtic hand drum, the *bodhrán*), I was able to build a loyal following. By the time I launched my online video tutorial course, Bodhrán Expert Platinum Membership, I had a waiting list of students chomping at the bit. They knew that if my free stuff was this good my paid program was going to be off the charts.

I used free tools such as YouTube to share my message. By leveraging social media (so people were bound to find me no matter where they were hanging out), I was able to drive all traffic to my website. This provided me with the opportunity to build a list so that I could send awesome free content to all my subscribers as well as promote my paid programs.

And then guess what happened?

During my second launch, I had my first $20,000 day! I can honestly say that I could never have experienced this success without the use of video. Think about it. If I was able to receive this kind of response from a super-small, extremely targeted niche such as the *bodhrán*, just imagine what you can do.

I'm going to teach you how to reach your global audience by demonstrating how the power of video (cloning yourself) combined with speaking from your core (your authentic self) can lead to financial abundance and a wealth of time and energy for you and your family.

What does it really mean to be "authentic"? For me, being authentic means:

1. Putting the focus on serving others.

2. Not trying to emulate other people. Be the best version of you!

3. Not worrying about what other people think (this gets a lot easier once you find your purpose).

4. Leaving your ego at the door (or laughing at her when she tries to take you down).

5. Speaking to the camera as if you're talking to your best friend.

6. Not comparing yourself to others.

7. Being unique.

8. Not being afraid or embarrassed about being ferociously passionate and enthusiastic about what inspires you.

Speaking from your core allows you to speak directly to someone else's heart. When you're authentic in your videos, you'll discover that people you've never met will feel as if they personally know you. When you show them a world of endless possibilities, they'll want to hang out with you because of your high-vibe energy and how uplifted they feel from your presence.

I get messages from students all the time saying that, when they're watching my training videos, they feel as if I'm right in the room with them, taking them by the hand through their learning journey. When they admit to speaking back to my videos (as if we're having a real life conversation) I can't help but smile because this is the exact desired outcome I hoped to accomplish. It's one of the biggest compliments they could give me.

Getting yourself to an authentic state of being should be your key objective. When people see you baring your soul on video, it gives them the freedom and permission to do the same. Once you're in the right mindset, people will be more likely to feel as if you're in the room with them, speaking directly to them. Pretty close to cloning, wouldn't you say?

For me, "cloning" yourself through video means recording one video that could reach thousands (or even millions) of people. This provides your subscribers with the luxury of learning from you at their convenience, no matter where they're located. It also gives them the opportunity to be able to watch your videos as many times as they like. Meanwhile, you might be off in another part of the world, sound asleep in your bed or busy taking your child to swimming lessons.

Take the following scenario as an example: If each of my 6,000 YouTube subscribers wanted a one-hour Skype lesson with me, that would mean I'd have to teach 35 hours/week, 48 weeks/year for almost 4 years before I could then begin second lessons with each of them.

Are you starting to see the potential of cloning yourself through video?

Without authenticity, you might as well be talking to a brick wall. This is why my chapter is titled "The Authentic Clone."

Chances are, if you're reading this right now, you're extremely passionate about something in your life. Do you have a talent or knowledge you want to share with the world but just don't know how? Well, you're in great company because there are all kinds of musicians, teachers, artists, coaches, writers, authors, etc., just like you who want to get their message out into the world and get paid for their expertise, but they don't know how to get started. I'm about to take the mystery out of how to reach your global audience and reward your talents.

Reaching Your Global Audience

To reach your global audience, and I'm talking about real people in the real world, you need to learn about the online world. Learning how to attract your ideal audience and how to "authentically clone" yourself through video will enable you to share your talents with the world via your products or services.

I can just hear you now: "This is easy for her to say. She could do it, but I couldn't."

Trust me. It definitely wasn't easy when I began my journey into the video world. Seriously, my very first video "Welcome to my YouTube channel" took 42 takes. And let me tell you, I felt like the biggest phony on the planet! But looking back, I now realize that was because I was still worried about what other people would think of me.

I know how crippling the thought of just standing in front of a video camera can be, with the red record button flashing like a beacon screaming "Everyone look at me!" Putting yourself out there for the whole world to see (and possibly criticize) can be so intimidating that fear can stop you in your tracks, before you even take that very first step.

There's never been a better time to get started. The online world is changing so rapidly that even those who actually understand what's going on are finding themselves on a constant learning curve. It's no wonder that people who feel they don't know anything about Internet marketing, product creation, and monetizing their talents feel like it's too late to jump on the bandwagon. Although the thought of technology scares us (and believe me, I'm speaking from personal experience), we don't have to look too far to find justifiable excuses that hold us back: "It's too hard," "It would take a lot of money," "I don't have the time," or "I don't like seeing myself on camera." The truth is, we can't afford NOT to be doing something about it.

If cost is your excuse, I'm happy to be the one to break it to you that the days where people spend thousands of dollars to create a website are thankfully over. Advances in online technology and marketing have made things easier and cheaper than ever before. If you think about it, this is awesome news for anyone who's just getting started online.

Through the power of the web you can now access billions of internet users. To this day, I have yet to spend a penny on advertisements promoting my programs and services. The new model is believing that you can do what you're passionate about for a living. You can monetize your talents, expertise, and skills in a way that can help more people than ever before and create your own financial abundance at the same time.

You see, I think all of our gifts are like music. They're out there, wanting to be played, and they're seeking expression through you. By you playing music, creating art, writing books, speaking on stage, teaching yoga—whatever it is that you are truly great at, no matter what level you're at—you're like a living, breathing conduit for this invisible "music" to come to life through you. Being the conduit for taking something from lifeless and silent to alive and heard by many is what living a passionate life is all about.

A few simple words you speak or write might just impact someone else's world the way Wayne Dyer's eight little words impacted mine when he said "Don't die with your music still inside you". It was like a switch flipped in my head, and I went from fearful to fearless in a heartbeat. You just know in that moment when you are following your dream that you are living your life on purpose. Don't worry, you'll know when it happens. It's the most burning desire you'll ever experience.

Here's a quick recap of how I started my journey into the online world. In November 2008, I didn't have a website. I didn't even know what a "list" was. My son was four years old, and I was trying to juggle a full-time music teaching career with family life. On top of all that, my husband and I were in the planning stages of knocking down our old house to build a new one. I pretty much felt like I was chasing my tail, constantly trying to keep up but never quite winning the race against time.

I was running the drumming programs at two private schools in Scotland and teaching *bodhrán* on the weekends through the Royal Scottish Academy Of Music and Drama. While getting the chance to teach drumming for a living was a dream come true for me, it got to the point that (because I was teaching so much) my voice was being strained to the max. I was told I might need surgery.

I love teaching so much that when I thought my voice might get so bad that I couldn't continue teaching, I became very afraid. I was forced to think outside the typical teaching box.

That's when my video-making journey began.

The first couple of videos were definitely the most challenging. It actually took quite a bit of practice and trial and error to "be myself" on camera. Sounds kind of weird, right? For me, regularly putting myself into that uncomfortable place of stepping in front of the camera and pressing the record button was how I got over myself.

Once I tapped into the "real me," I knew I was on the right path with making videos. I felt such confidence in this knowing that I didn't even care that my voice was super croaky. I sounded like an 80-year-old man who smoked 2 packs of cigarettes every day of his life. So although I was experiencing some doubts and insecurities, my excitement to get started helped overcome my fear.

Here's where it all switched on a dime for me: Once I changed my mindset and shifted my focus from thoughts such as "What will they think?", "How do I look on camera?", or "What if someone leaves a bad comment?" to "How can I serve?" it got a heck of a lot easier.

Top tip: Creating videos that will really help others by putting the focus on serving the world (rather than serving yourself) is like having your very own magic wand. It makes stepping in front of the camera not only effortless, but fun! It sounds almost too simple, but it works.

The ACT Formula

Ask + Create + Transform = Authentic Clone

Step 1: Ask

1. Ask for inspiration. Still your mind and ask "How can I serve and make a difference in this world—even to just one person?"

2. Don't try to come up with the answer yourself. Have a little blind faith and wait for inspired thoughts to come to you.

3. Write down the inspired thoughts that pop into your head (don't censor/edit).

4. Put a reminder on your phone that pops up every day asking "How can I serve?"

Step 2: Create

1. Create valuable free content videos and post them on YouTube.

2. Don't hold back!

3. Give some of your best tips, advice, or lessons that can get instant results for your viewers.

4. Make the advice very clear, simple and easy for them to implement so they are more likely to get instant gratification or results and will thank you for it.

Step 3: Transform

1. Accept that your talent/product/service can transform people's lives.

2. I know what you're thinking: "But someone else is already doing that." Yes, someone might have already said it before, but the way you say it and explain it will resonate with someone in a way that finally allows them to truly "hear" it.

3. What you have to say makes a difference.

When you're in the "How can I serve?" mindset, you'll often find yourself in front of the video camera and something will come out of your mouth and you'll think "Oh, that's really quite clever. I didn't even know I knew that." You actually come up with better creative work that will impact people's lives in a bigger way when you come from this frame of mind.

I believe our gifts and talents aren't ours to keep. Leaving your legacy, while you're still living, is easier than you could ever imagine. It's also your duty to do just that.

If you're inspired to learn more, visit me at www.MichelleStewart.com.

Lori Latimer

At the age of 48, Lori found herself divorced and at a crossroads in her life. She realized she could stay on the path of "settling," or she could create a new life. As a speaker, scientific hand analyst, and life coach she now inspires others who are at a crossroads to find their purpose and choose their direction. Lori lives a life she loves in Atlanta near her 2 sons and 2 little grandsons.

Website:	http://www.lorilatimer.com
Facebook:	http://www.facebook.com/loriannlatimer
Facebook:	http://www.facebook.com/lorilatimercoach
Twitter:	@lorilatimer
Pinterest:	http://www.pinterest.com/lorilatimer/
LinkedIn:	http://www.linkedin.com/in/lorilatimer

TIP 19

Create a Hot Mama Life You Love After 50

by Lori Latimer

It was January 2008. There it was, looming large and coming closer by the day. That birthday, the one so many people dread: The big 5-0 was just two short years away. My husband and I had been together for almost 11 years. I had two sons: one married with a little baby boy of his own, and one in his senior year of high school. Things in my marriage had been spiraling downward for some time. Looking back, I realize things started spiraling downward even before we were married. But it wasn't my first marriage. Did I really want to walk away and start over again at 48?

I grew up living the American childhood dream. My dad owned his own business and my mom stayed at home. My younger brother and I went to private school for a while. We took some fantastic vacations, often several times a year. I grew up thinking I'd be like my mom and get married and not have to work. Reality proved to be a very different story.

As I looked at my life at 48, I was working a full-time job for someone else that provided me a good income, but left me unfulfilled in so many ways, and I was ready to leave another marriage. I will never forget sitting in an apartment leasing office one cold day in January 2008, tears streaming down my face as I signed the lease. I didn't feel remotely close to being a Hot Mama. Instead, I felt like a failure.

I knew somewhere deep inside me that this was a pivotal moment in my life. I was at a crossroads: I could stay on the path I was on, which meant I was signing a slow death sentence for my soul, or I could stop settling for whatever happened to come my way. The latter meant taking a new direction in my life, one I hadn't taken before. The choice—while anything but easy—was also crystal clear. It was time, *my time*, to create the life I wanted to live the rest of my life. But how?

While pondering that question, I kept getting stumped over the "how." Then one day a close friend asked me a life-changing question: "What brings you joy?" That's when the real fun began! See, I had no earthly idea what brought me joy. Sounds crazy, I know (but I'll bet many of you can relate!). I realized I was living on autopilot, giving a response that wasn't about *me*, but rather about roles I'd played all my life, labels I'd attached to myself—as a mother, grandmother, wife, daughter, sister, friend, paralegal…the list was endless. But those labels were all about who I was *in relation to other people*. I knew that, to find the answers about who I am at a soul level, I had to strip away all those labels that had defined me for so many years.

Then my not-so-friendly inner critic came to visit. The first thing she said was, "Are you crazy? You can't do that! You're almost 50! *You're too old*."

In that instant, I made a decision. I chose to take a new path, a new direction, one that I'd never taken before, one that still leaves me breathless, wondering *is this really my life?*

I was at that crossroads just 5 years ago. Today, I'm happily single. I'm no longer an employee for someone else. I do freelance paralegal work while building my own business, one that satisfies me in the deepest places of my soul. So how did I get from my own personal crossroads to where I am today?

I did it by getting clear on the life I want to live the rest of my life and taking what at times were some very scary steps toward it—and you can, too! If you're at your own crossroads and ready to create a life you want to live, here are 5 steps to get you on a new and exciting path. They may appear very simple, but don't let that fool you—they aren't always easy.

1. Awareness

Call it mindfulness, awareness, or waking up, but one of my first steps was becoming aware that I'd lived most (or maybe all) of my life on autopilot. Living on autopilot leads to settling for things that happen to come along rather than creating what your heart and soul yearn for. That first awareness led to becoming aware of so many things—both what I wanted as well as what I was no longer willing to settle for. Here are two quick ways to become more aware:

- **Take a different route** to work, the grocery store, or anywhere you drive regularly. How many times do you arrive at a frequent destination with no recollection of part of the drive there? Taking a different route will increase your awareness and get you out of the autopilot mode.

- **Mix it up**—your routine, that is! If you normally work out in the morning, try doing it in the afternoon. Listen to a different type of music. Try a new restaurant. We often get stuck in a routine that becomes a rut, which leads to living on autopilot. Mixing up your routine is another way to bring new awareness to your life.

2. Solitude

Our world today is so noisy and chaotic. We're constantly plugged in. Step into an elevator and, instead of people looking at one another and perhaps even saying hello, chances are that everyone is looking at their smartphones. We have 500 channels on television, movies on demand, and access to practically anyone and anything all the time. The upside of this is we're able to connect with people on the other side of the globe and meet amazing people we weren't able to meet just a few years ago. The downside is that it allows us to avoid really being still. Spending quiet time alone can be one of the most difficult things to do, but it's also one of the quickest ways to finding out who you really are and what you really want. It gives you time to reflect on your past and see what worked and what didn't work.

Turn off the phone, TV, email, and Internet. Close your eyes, and for three minutes simply focus on your breath. Each inhale and each exhale will bring you more in touch with your body, your spirit, and ultimately your deepest desires.

3. Journal

I know, I know, you've heard this so many times. You may even do it. But get a beautiful new journal. If you already journal regularly, do it in a different way. Switch the time of day you do it. Get some fun colored markers. I used to get all caught up in doing it "perfectly." Once I started writing without editing myself, I was amazed at what came out. So just free write and don't edit it. If you've never journaled before, start with something simple. Write a list of 3 to 5 things you're grateful for each night before you go to bed and challenge yourself to write different things each night. After 21 days, look back to see if any themes or patterns have emerged. Do the same thing with your dreams. This can be a good indication of some of your innermost desires.

4. Movement

This is a fun one! We live very sedentary lifestyles. As a result, we've become very disconnected from our bodies. So turn on some music you love and just dance! It doesn't matter what you look like, just move your body. To tune into what you want and desire, you have to get in touch with all your senses. Dancing is one of the quickest and easiest ways to do that.

5. Hand Analysis

I had no idea what this even was when I made my hand prints and mailed them off to be analyzed in May 2010. Little did I know that it would completely change my life. Your hands contain a wealth of information, including your life purpose, your life lesson/challenge, and other potential gifts, talents, and challenges. The left brain part of me loves that it's based in science (which makes it incredibly accurate), and the right brain part of me loves the artistry in blending all of it together. Are you a spiritual teacher? A successful artist in the spotlight? A leader in the community? Maybe an inspirational communicator? Your hands hold the answers and will give you a direction for creating a life that will fulfill you at a soul level. Helping others find all this information in their hands now brings me so much joy.

Life always brings challenges. We can choose to look at them as problems, or we can choose to look at them as opportunities and lessons for soul growth. I invite you to look at your path and ask yourself if you're living on autopilot or if you're living on purpose. You might be surprised at the answer. I know I was.

Is the new path always easy? Am I there yet? Of course not! I know it's a journey. I'm on an ever-winding path that will always bring new twists and turns to my life, but I know that it's a path of my conscious choosing, which is what makes it so satisfying and fulfilling at a soul level. That's what makes it joyful and f-u-n!

Barbara J Eisele,
MC, NCC, PCC

Barbara is the founder of Life Transformations, Now. She has many years of formal education, yet her greatest learning happened in the "classroom of life." She has been a nurse and counselor and is currently an ICF certified coach, consultant, speaker, wife, and grandmother. Women today feel a deep yearning for "something more," something they often can't name. Barbara's passion is leading women to discover and create a life that fully expresses their authentic brilliance.

Website: www.lifetransformationsnow.com
Email: barb@lifetransformationsnow.com
Facebook: www.facebook.com/beisele
Facebook: www.facebook.com/LifeTransformationsNow.
Twitter: @barbeisele.
Pinterest: www.pinterest.com/barbaraeisele
Phone: 520-977-0562

TIP 20

Discovering Your Authentic Brilliance

by Barbara J Eisele

"I can't go on," I said to my husband, "my life isn't worth living!"

I was despondent as I sat crying, my head in my hands, rocking back and forth, as he tried his best to comfort me. For the very first time in my life I was unable to see any future worth living. We were facing a foreclosure on our dream home, which we had spent months designing down to the last detail of floors, doors, and finishes. What was most intense was the humiliation I felt as a result of this. It challenged my core values of integrity and responsibility. I had always said I am responsible for my life and the choices I make, but this? My belief of not being good enough and my core fear of being alone were now overwhelming me, and I could not see a reason to live.

My husband queried me about what my clients would do if I wasn't here. I told him there were plenty of great coaches that they could find. He kept his cool after he asked me "What about our relationship?" and I told him I thought he could find a better wife. Then he asked, "What about our children and grandchildren?" I told him that I had done my job, and our children would be fine. However, when I thought about our grandchildren, I came up short. In that moment, the darkness cracked enough and I realized there were two little souls where I made a difference. I sat in the conundrum of these two precious children needing me and having no idea how I was going to put together some semblance of a respectable life. How would I hold my head high with friends, business colleagues, and clients?

I was surprised at my profound reaction to losing our home. After all, in 2012 I wasn't the only American finding foreclosure the reality of their lives. But this was more than our lovely home; it was the loss of my identity. I didn't know who I was anymore, and the only thread I had to hang on to was the difference I made in the lives of my grandchildren. I had spent time with clients exploring how we aren't our address, our clothes, our bank account, or any other worldly possession, but my emotional reality was exposed on this dark August morning.

After doing extensive transformational personal growth work for 30 years and coaching for almost half of those, this situation left me asking hard questions: Who am I? Why am I here? What am I to do with my life? No stranger to this inquiry, I was shocked at how much of my identity was wrapped up in the material world. This showed me how much I bought into what society says I "should" have, who I "should" be, and what constitutes success. It was stunning how victimized I felt by my circumstances.

Our perception determines what and how we see things in the world. Acknowledging my deep despair, feeling the thread of hope provided by my grandchildren, and experiencing my husband's deep, supportive love lifted me to a different place. Our children were amazingly supportive despite their own sense of confusion, loss, and fear.

I leaned heavily on three dear girlfriends who were unconditionally supportive and loving. With them I ripped off the mask of "I'm handling everything just fine" and spoke vulnerably about what I was experiencing. This tapped into my deep fear of being alone, but I knew that the courage to speak the truth to myself and those that loved me was part of this journey.

Our two precious grandchildren provided the essential ingredients of fun, lightheartedness, and hope.

I knew I didn't want to try and recreate the life I had been living. This was my chance to express the Authentic Me, but first I had to get to know who she was. I turned to practices that had supported me in the past. I had to start where I was. Serendipitously I was given some books that inspired me. They all reinforced that the Barbara who yearned to emerge from this "dark night of the soul" was already deep inside me. It was time to discover more aspects of my Soul Self and nurture her to full expression.

Each morning I wrote in a beautiful journal that a dear friend sent me. This took my fears and confusion out of my head and put them on paper. It was important for me to set aside enough time to write because there is always a point where my perception shifts and insights magically flow from my pen.

Reading a dear friend's unpublished book manuscript reminded me that others have walked through a "dark night of the soul" and emerged healthier, stronger, and—most of all—wiser.

I reopened my gratitude journal and wrote 5 new gratitudes each morning and evening. The support my loving husband gave me and the hope my grandchildren provided topped my list each day. Being in gratitude always brings my attention to the sweet spot of *now*.

I meditated using a process that is designed to re-wire the brain's neuropathways. Old ways of thinking and doing must be transformed to bring forth new behaviors.

Slowing down, using the food budget funds to buy myself flowers, and enjoying a glass of nice red wine were simple pleasures of the day that stopped me from ruminating on the past or worrying about the future.

The pilgrimage to discovering our Authentic Self, who we really are, is not walked by the faint of heart. Maybe that's why so many of us find ourselves in circumstances that devastate us physically, emotionally, financially, or spiritually before we reach the point of no return and put our feet on the path, searching for the truth of who we really are.

The inquiry to discover our Authentic Self can be initiated before we feel like our life is falling apart. If we listen, our soul has been nagging to be heard. Its voice might be a persistent desire, an emotion, or a bodily experience that we tolerate and push aside to keep going. Does any of this sound familiar?

Do any of the following resonate with you?

- You are restless, looking for something for the "next chapter" of your life.
- You find yourself asking some version of "is this all there is?"
- You are very "successful" in your career but aren't fulfilled by it.
- The same issues keep showing up, leaving you feeling exhausted, irritable, resentful, or resigned.
- Your relationships lack meaning or are in turmoil.
- You have experienced a major loss that has shaken you to your core.

Getting Started

The following questions inspired me during my deeply reflective times. I believe they might be helpful to you as well. It might have been a long time since you spent time with your Soul Self. This is a dynamic process; let it unfold organically. Take a deep breath. Shake off any tension in your body. Approach each one with curiosity. You might experience a wide range of emotions from delight and surprise, possibly sadness or confusion, perhaps inspiration or deep peace.

It's important to feel the emotion of each answer in your body. Name it as you feel it. Where does the emotion live in your body? Get to know all of you. Write your reflections in your journal.

- What do you love?
- Where do you shine?
- What do you admire most about your work or personal life?
- What are you passionate about in the world? Why?
- When do you feel that you can take on anything and achieve it?
- Is there something that is "calling you"? Have you been ignoring it?
- What feeds your soul? (e.g., a bath, music, beauty, being in nature, making a difference for others).

It may be new and a bit strange to focus on your strengths, your gifts, your talents, your Authentic Brilliance, "who you really are". I recommend you make a date with her on a regular basis and get to be very dear friends. Experience the positive emotions of being fully and powerfully You.

To really start to shift and live from your Authentic Brilliance, action is required. Yep, the rubber has to meet the road.

- Look through your answers. Choose one thing that brings forth an emotion you would choose to live in. Maybe it's really stepping into an area where you shine or maybe it's time to take a baby step on something you are passionate about.

- Use your imagination to visualize expressing your Authentic Brilliance. Get a very clear picture of you fully expressing this gift. How would you stand, dress, and speak? Feel the emotion throughout your body.

- Decide what action you can do today—yes, today—to get started. There is no action too small. Put it in your calendar. Make it a priority. Keep the promise to yourself to do it and start trusting yourself to express your Authentic Brilliance.

I send you blessings for this journey. The world needs your gifts and is waiting for you to bring your Authentic Brilliance into full expression. We are the ones we have been waiting for and the time is now.

A complimentary workbook that goes into this exercise in depth is available at www.lifetransformationsnow.com/HotMama

Christine Marmoy

Christine Marmoy, innovative global speaker, creative edge marketing mentor, and dream team designer passionately shares her message of hope, excitement, and inspired action worldwide to empower women to unleash their innovative edge to boost visibility, build credibility, and profit successfully in business. Christine is also the compiler and publisher of the international bestseller *Success in (High) Heels.* Her own book, *These Dreams Are Made for Walking,* an inspirational book that helps women (and men) step into their real power to make their dreams a reality and to be unstoppable in life and business through her Success Workout, is due out in October 2013. Christine reveals her BIRTH IT formula to help business owners (and others) release their creative genius and awaken their dreams to achieve wild success. Christine works with women who desire to boldly expand their reach, make a bigger impact, increase their influence, and turn their ideas into daily bank account deposits.

Website: www.coachingandsuccess.com
Website: www.thewomensedgemag.com
Website: www.successinhighheels.com
Facebook: www.facebook.com/coachingandsuccess
Pinterest: www.pinterest.com/christinemarmoy

TIP 21

But Mum, Dad, Aren't You Supposed to Show Me the World?

by Christine Marmoy

Throw your dreams into space like a kite,
and you do not know what it will bring back,
a new life, a new friend, a new love, a new country.

When you were a child, your world was basically defined by your parents; as you grew up, your siblings took over part of that role, followed by your teachers who taught you way more than the textbooks asked them to—and most of the time they didn't even acknowledge it. As you grew still older, you made your own way through life, picking up limiting beliefs along the way through experiences, deceptions, rejections, and even failures. Now if that particular rejection hit a nerve from a past belief deeply rooted in your childhood, it's easy to understand the principle of reinforcement. You simply added a new layer to the belief structure.

Ever since I was a kid, I have always loved traveling, which might explain why I have moved so many times and initially chose a profession that required frequent travelling or moving around. Although my dad was an immigrant, I never got to travel much with my parents. We never went back to his homeland as a family. I definitely had the travel bug in my blood, but for some reason, my mum was the one who couldn't stand traveling, so we ended up staying at home year after year.

With my first job, I got to travel to Switzerland, Amsterdam, and Cologne, which in reality were not that far away, but for me meant "going away." Although traveling for work could be tiring and challenging at times, I knew I needed that pace to feel alive.

Another belief that I have jealously guarded to myself for years is that change means instability and instability means immaturity, unworthiness, or unfaithfulness. Ever since my early childhood of playing in a pretend world, I have never stopped changing; I fell in love with change at first sight! Can you imagine what it was like to be living and growing up in a family for whom change was perceived as instability? As I like change, it means I have different perfumes, (way too) many pairs of shoes, a load of handbags, and numerous outfits. I don't keep the same car for very long. All this just because I like to change things once in a while, including rearranging furniture 2 to 3 times a year, if I don't actually move from one year to the next! My mum used to tell me that I was really unstable just because I had different perfumes or because I changed my hairstyle. Why would I be unstable just because I like change?

Anyway, this belief ended up with me staying with a nasty husband for 10 years and sticking to a corporate job for 20 years. For almost 2 decades I managed to include change in my life, but in a way that was imposed upon me by my external environment. I moved a lot for work. The truth was that I had somewhat chosen that job because it could provide me with the change I needed so badly to feel alive, without having to take on the responsibility of deciding to do it in the first place.

Like many of you, I grew up in a very "normal" family with its fair share of limitations, restrictions, and fears, so when I finally did decide to take the leap and create my first business, I had to fight very hard with myself because I remembered what I had learned: "You don't make money when you work for yourself." I chose the completely opposite path, as if I wanted to prove to my parents that they were wrong. Little did I know at the time that you cannot succeed for the wrong reasons. This is why I'm not going to tell you that it was fantastic, that I had clients lining up waiting to work with me, or that I made 6 figures in 6 months. In fact it was quite the opposite. I struggled every day. I lost sleep. At one point I didn't even understand why people were not interested in what I had to offer as my programs and products were exactly what they needed.

In theory I was obviously right, but the reality was quite different. This is when I came to understand that there was a tangible discrepancy between what clients need and what they want. I was offering them what they needed, not what they wanted. No wonder my offers were a miss.

It was hard at the time, particularly because the first thing my parents, my friends, and even my kids told me when I decided to walk away from the corporate world to create my own business sounded nothing like support; in fact, it felt as if they were taking great delight in trying to bring reason into my crazy head. They all thought I had lost my mind, and maybe I did. So what? Nothing would ever happen if I remained in the same situation. Something had to give, something had to change. I could feel it in my stomach, in my heart, in my very bones. The million-dollar question was what was "it"? Was it my job? Would opening my own business be the solution? Was it my house? Could moving be the solution? Was it my marriage? Heck no, I didn't want to change that; I was happy given the situation. After numerous sleepless nights, I decided to throw myself headfirst into the cold, deep, dark waters of business and see what I could get out of it. I had an MBA, which had never really served any purpose for me other than ensuring a nice paycheck, so it was about time to monetize and gain something from this expensive learning.

What I didn't really grasp at the beginning was that this "business idea" of mine was the best idea I've ever had—not because it brought me in money, I was successful, or I only needed to work 4 hours a day. No, that would have been too easy. It was the best idea because it was in fact a catalyst for what was lying ahead of me on the path to my success. You see, like everybody else, I needed to come to terms with closure in certain aspects of my life. I needed to get rid of many limiting beliefs before I could even feel worthy of success. So yes, in between the lines of the balance sheet, this endeavor was a success, even if my accountant would disagree if you asked him. We are all human beings and, as such, we learn mostly through adversity when our backs are up against the wall. In this case, the wall was my beliefs. I had to pull that wall down brick by brick, and the more bricks I piled up on the floor, the more difficult it became to grab the next one and pull it down.

You know something? It's nerve-wracking, tiring, frustrating, and challenging to deconstruct 30 years of brain washing. Willingness and dedication just aren't enough. You really need to work at it, all day, every day, with your last breath. But all I can tell you is that it's worth it. If I had to do it all again, I'd do it in the blink of an eye. However, to be totally honest with you, I would now take a few shortcuts and I wouldn't fight with myself as much to drop useless habits, like smoking. Yes, I quit smoking because of my business. Isn't that amazing? In fact I made a deal with myself. At one point I asked myself how I could succeed at my business if I couldn't even quit smoking. This was for me an epiphany. I'm not saying that I couldn't have succeeded because I smoked, all I'm saying is that I needed to test my willpower. I needed to answer one simple question: Do I really want this to work?

What would you give up that is difficult for you so you can make room for your future success? Cigarettes were my answer. But don't think for one minute that it was easy; it was actually the most difficult thing I have ever done in my life, because I liked smoking (and still do, by the way). You have no idea how many times I wished I had a cigarette (albeit less and less now as I realized a while ago that meditation is even better). I can recall a Wednesday night when I was staring at my computer, contemplating the debris of what was once my business. Two days before the launch of the second issue of the *Women's Edge Magazine*, all our sites had gone down, shattered into little pieces by hackers. We had to rebuild everything, and I couldn't get in touch with my hosting company. That night, if I had had a cigarette next to me, I would have smoked it! It wouldn't have helped the situation, I grant you that, but at least I would have fulfilled one of my weaknesses, and that type of sin can be so tempting.

The second reason why having this business idea was a blessing is the fact that I realized I could see the world through my business. My business would show me the world. With today's technology, you can travel around the globe without even leaving your office chair—and that's what I do. Today, I have clients all over the world, so every day I travel to wonderful places. Through my speaking, I'm able to visit remote places that I didn't even know existed. I meet new people, experience different cultures, and get to learn so much from all the people I encounter in my work.

My parents didn't show me the world, but by removing old and undesirable beliefs, I freed up my business and in return it gave me the opportunity to see the world.

It may be hard to disregard the things you were told by your dad, your mom, your uncle, or whoever that particular loved one was, to stand up and start walking the lonely path of your own beliefs. However, that's all there is to it. At some point in life, if your happiness and success really matter to you, you'll do whatever it takes. Getting rid of useless beliefs is a major stepping stone in this crucial process.

Here is a small and simple (from the outside) exercise to do:

Take a sheet of paper and draw 4 columns.

Column 1: My limiting beliefs

List all the limiting beliefs you hold in your head and in your heart (keep it open as you'll find new ones almost every day).

Column 2: Who gave it to me?

Just write the name of the person who you think or know gave you this belief (it doesn't matter why).

Column 3: Does this belief still serve me?

Answer yes or no.

Column 4: I create my new belief

Reformulate a positive belief that resonates with you. Remember it has to be stated in the present and in a positive way.

The last part of the exercise is a little affirmation to thank whoever gave you the beliefs you decided to change:

Dear (fill in the blank), Thank you for having offered me this belief at a point in my life when you felt I needed it. I release it now because I have grown up and do not need it anymore. Now I create my own based on where I am right now on my true path. I love you.

TIP 22

The Maya Story

by Christine Marmoy

*Those who dream by day are cognizant of many things
which escape those who dream only by night.*
–Edgar Allan Poe

"Oh no, Christine, why did you cut up my new magazine! How many times do I have to tell you not to touch the magazines on the table, I haven't read them yet!" I probably knew that, but in my defense, I was only about 5 years old, so what could my mom expect from a wild-spirited 5-year-old like me?

I might have only been 5, but there was something I could spend hours doing: making my own mag using my mom's magazines (usually the ones she had already read, of course). I used to cut the titles out because I liked the colors, the shape, or the font. Now remember, I was no genius, so no, I couldn't read at that age. I was using recycled paper from my dad to make the pages, cutting out everything that appealed to my eyes—titles, pictures, columns of text—just because I liked them. My grandma used to buy me markers in all different colors, all types of pencils, glitter glues, stickers (or whatever we could find at the time), and I would use them to create my own magazine, without understanding one single word of what was written. So you could easily have found an ad for a car in the middle of an article talking about what dish to cook on your 10th anniversary and then read through the end of an anonymous article about where to travel safely on a low budget.

But it was my dream, my magazine and especially my message. When was the last time you recognized the message you had to share with the world—with your world?

I was the elder of 2 girls. In fact, we were only 24 months apart—not enough to understand each other, but too much to hang out with each other. My dad was self-employed: He had his own car dealership and repair shop. My mom, like most women at that time, was a housewife. Dare I say that I grew up in a household where work equaled money right down to the last penny? My dad had a very simple belief, which I had to strip myself of years later: To avoid paying too much in taxes, he had to keep it low key, and by low key I mean not making too much money. So, yes, I grew up with the belief that it was better to make just enough to get by, but not too much otherwise the money would be taken away from me, no matter what! Talk about a limiting belief! It's a suicidal belief for any entrepreneur out there, yet I became just that.

How many of you are still holding on to this type of belief today while having no evidence of the truth it is supposed to support? Do me a favor and decide today to take a very strong look at what you believe in to the point that you'd fight for it. Make the wonderful decision to only stick to what you stand for and just throw everything else into the trash bin, even if that means rejecting what your dad told you for so many years. This is the best thing you'll ever do for yourself, your dreams, and your coming success. Start by living up to the promise you make to yourself and make sure you only keep what can serve you for the greatest good.

Do you remember the voice you heard when you were a child? Some called it their invisible friend, others called it their child voice. Me? I called it Maya. Why Maya? Just because that voice I had in my head was uncensored, undistracted, and uncolored by what grown-ups thought of the truth. That voice spoke out from my heart, and I remember feeling like everything was possible. Do you remember that feeling? Do you remember what it feels like, as if nothing can stop you, that once you have an idea, the only thing you need to see it through is to just do something about it? Just like the Mayan people created their own civilization, my Maya created my world as a little girl. Besides, I love the name, and if my last kid had been a girl, I would have named her Maya, but that is beside the point here.

So what's that story? What is my Maya story? When I was a little girl, I used to think that when I grew up I'd be more than just human. I didn't know what it meant but for me at the time, more meant being something different than just human. I know, it's funny how kids can see the human race as such a small achievement, isn't it? Now each time I wanted to have or do something, I used to have this dialogue with my Maya: How can I get this? How do I get that? What should I do to be able to get this? Who should I ask to do that? And usually the answers would come in the form of positive, inspiring, and motivating orders: Why don't you try this?

I remember one afternoon visiting my grandma. I saw in the window of a shoe store the prettiest, most amazing pair of ballerina shoes. My mom had just bought me new ones, so I knew that my chances of getting another brand new pair of shoes—and expensive ones at that—were very slim. The next thing I remember was that the soles of my shoes came unglued in two places, so my mom decided to take me to that store and get me a new pair. That day I said to myself: "I can get anything I want as long as I really want it!"

Who is your Maya? What was that voice you could hear when you were just a kid? We all had one, even if you don't recognize it right away. Just try and pause for a moment and go back in time. Imagine yourself in your parents' living room, in the kitchen, in the garden, or even in your own room: What emotions are welling up inside you? What voice can you hear? Who was that voice? What is that voice saying?

Remember, your Maya is that voice which used to think that you could do, be, or have anything you wished as long as you wanted it. It's that uncensored, positive, loving, daring, fearless voice that you heard in your head and in your heart when you were not old enough to be told otherwise.

That voice was the voice of unlimited possibilities, the source, the beginning. It represented everything that could be. It's the same voice that once told you to get up and see what's on the other side. Yes, it's the voice that motivated you to stand up straight and whispered that you could walk if you wanted to. It's the voice that carried you through misfortunes because you had no idea that consequences even existed. It's the voice that announced the playfulness of life to its fullest. It's the voice that existed before you could even acknowledge there was a voice!

Close your eyes and listen! Where is that voice now?

Now that you remember the voice, how can you reconnect with it so it can guide you every day into making every decision feel tinged with confidence, making you feel more comfortable with the notion of "course correction" because it is a natural part of the process?

This may sound a bit "out there," but believe me, it works so well that I changed my life by 180°, applying it to everything I do in my business to the point that it transformed my entire life. I'm writing an entire book about it, and as this book is being released to the public, I'll be teaching this (and many other things) in my workshops all over Europe.

But don't take my word for it, just try it and see for yourself.

Early in the morning, when everybody else is still sleeping (yes, you'll have to get up early) or in the evening, in the stillness of the night, find a place in your house where you know you won't be disturbed, where you won't annoy anybody. Mentally dedicate this place to your soul work.

Take a sheet of paper and answer the following questions:

1. When did I feel in touch with my little voice? Recall past experiences, feelings, and emotions. You might not be sure if it was initiated by your Maya, but at this stage you can easily assume it was. It will make the entire process much easier.

2. What was the context? Where were you—at home, at a relatives, on vacation?

3. What did you feel at the time? What was the strongest emotion? Feel it in your heart and body; both of them will remember, no matter when the event occurred.

4. What was the reason for the request? What was the request?

5. What was the result? How close was it to what you expected or wanted?

6. What was the emotion that you felt once you realized that your Maya had not only listened, but also responded positively?

Now do the same exercise for all the other events you remember. You don't have to do everything at once; you could easily just do one event a day.

Once you are done with remembering the proof of your Maya's existence, it's time to reconnect, open the line, call her in some strange and weird ways. Take a nice little notebook, one that you feel good just by looking at and handling it, and start talking to your Maya through writing.

You might be wondering what to write about or that what you write is simply rubbish. You are entitled to think whatever you like, but remember that this has worked for me and many other people I shared this exercise with, so maybe—just maybe—trying it out and giving it a fair shot is not that farfetched.

One point to remember: You need to give it an honest try; anything less than 30 days is not really considered an honest try.

Try it, then email me to tell me all the things that changed in your life. Believe me, it is really powerful

Conclusion

Did you cry a lot? Did you giggle or laugh with some chapters? I sure do hope so!

I thought about this conclusion for a long time, considering what I wanted you to remember the most or what I wanted you to get the most from after reading all these stories. My answer focused on 2 words: experience and self. In other words, I hope you got to experience the transformation of your own self (or at least I hope you felt the process starting).

As women, we seem fragile, sensitive (or too sensitive), naive, weak, and many other things to the outside world; in some countries, the perception is even worse. However, when you scratch the surface, if you dare look at what is nestled beneath the very thin surface, you get to see another side, another face. You see resilience, strength, courage, love, generosity, brilliance, integrity, and honesty—qualities that sometimes you work very hard to hide because someone once told you that they were not to be shown or because you were raised in a way that demonstrating resilience only meant lack of respect.

In these final words, I'm begging you to go stand in front of a mirror and look deeply into the eyes of your heart. What do you see?

A strong, beautiful, and self-confident woman.

Congratulations, you discovered YOU!

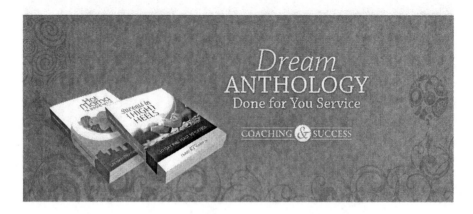

Do you dream of being published?

What I enjoy the most about my business is being able to collaborate with so many different women all over the world. And the best part? When I get to help them organize their very own collaborative work— that is where my real talent lies.

Without doubt, a book is The Asset to have to increase your visibility tenfold, gain instant credibility, and increase your clientele.

So if you want to turn your dream of publishing your own anthology book into reality, get in touch with me and I'll show you how. Together we can accomplish this in 90 days, cost-free, going through everything from A to Z—including how you can actually make money right from the very start.

Sounds good?

Then email me at christine@coachingandsuccess.com

Have a wonderful and successful life!

Christine Marmoy

The End!

Other books published
by Marketing for Coach, Ltd.
(Christine Marmoy)

Success in (High) Heels,
compiled by
Christine Marmoy

**Network to Increase
Your Net Worth,**
compiled by Toni Coleman-Brown

Survivor to Thriver,
compiled by Kate Gardner
(to be released)

Bold is Beautiful,
compiled by Kim Boudreau Smith
(to be released)

**Living Without Limitations – 30 Mentors
to Rock your World,**
compiled by Anita Sechesky
(to be released)

CPSIA information can be obtained at www.ICGtesting.com
Printed in the USA
LVOW06s1423161013

356947LV00013B/102/P